MW01231456

Aggression, Self Concept and Motor Ability of Sports Persons

KANKANWADI MALLAPPA

LIST OF CONTENTS

List of Contents

List of Table

List of Graphs

LIST OF TABLES

LIST OF GRAPHS

CHAPTER-I

INTRODUCTION

Sports are entertainment just as competition and are viewed as a component of one's life. They are existed as such through the ages. The word before long is gotten from two words 'dis' and 'doorman' signifying "diverting from work". At the point when we discuss spots, we unquestionably call attention to such inventive exercises which are unwinding in nature and which are accomplished for looking for "joy as it were". Essentially sports are singular exercises conceived out of regular desire for development however now-a-days at that point; is a propensity for, genuine and consolidated practice between different associations and between the individuals from the group. Sports are a vital part of human just as creature life. A playful kid is a solid kid. A playful grown-up is a casual, free and upbeat individual, not pointlessly grieved by these considerations and eroding tensions of world.

Truth be told sports, in the more extensive point of view, mean joy just as competition in sports; competition has become extreme and all people and country are endeavoring exceptionally difficult to acquire incomparability over others. Olympics and other world competitions may stand declaration to this reality. Sports fields are no more delight resorts, they are not the advertisers of worldwide fraternity and kindness, despite the fact that everyone .worried about sports guarantees so yet they have become field of merciless competitions where every individual is exceptionally energetic by his political bosses to "win" no matter what. This has come about in to various risky circumstances. Presently sports have become an incredibly perplexing wonder. Cohen [1973] believes that the pith of current game - is a social structure, as such which requests and is made conceivable by an exceptional handling of un-social driving forces. "Sports has been portrayed as" the silt of a most finely disseminated aggregate contempt encouraged in athletic challenges' According to this perspective, sports competition is only the "brutality of the refined man" or compelled choppiness.

The player let himself go, with in a genuine code of lead as he would not challenge to do anyplace, and yet in sports has set off on a thorough competition in research on human physiology, genetics, psychology and so on and associated fields so more prospects of dominating and "Winning" could be investigated. In actuality, marvelous changes have happened in the utilization of strategies for educating, training, instructing and taking care of sportsmen. Increasingly more specialization is sneaking in and now it's anything but a drop in the bucket for ever, become a top class competitor without going through thorough scientific training in a particular occasion.

In the light of the verifiable information, sports have not to be seen as a simple low maintenance yet as amazingly complex social issues, hereditary blessing, by and large great climate and the softly particular training go to make an individual athletes or players of some retribution. This is the motivation behind why mental parts of sports or "game psychology" have become a particularly difficult and fascinating field of study and examination.

Psychology of Sport

Psychology of game is a part of psychology that analyzes different parts of sports exercises and actual culture. It additionally contemplates the psychological parts of the competitor; character. It creates demonstrative strategies for choosing people of explicit games and powerful training technique, Sports psychology looks at the competitor clairvoyant states in different complex circumstances. Sports psychology is likewise intended to build up the psychological establishments of brandishing abilities by showing ideal Locomotor propensities and appropriate control one's body and by cultivating the competitor's resolution and all round advancement.

Current sports psychology has expanded extensively from the early spotlight on engine learning, discernment and bio-mechanics. John Salmela remembers a rundown for which the experts list their significant zones of interest in the field. The most rundown incorporates engine expertise mastering, character tension, and stress, struggle and competition, symbolism training, unwinding training, consideration training, inspiration, socialization, improvement, group building, play and relaxation, mental training, instructing, advising and wellness. The particular sports centralizations of these experts range right from moves to baseball and b-ball and from soccer and fencing to volleyball, tennis, golf, games and numerous others. A precise data of sports psychology is that it is quickly developing and quickly broadening its zones of use alongside this development can be discovered a reclassifying of the topic, strategies, and thoughts of the field.

The fundamental meaning of the sports psychology is "an investigation of conduct as it identifies with sports and athletes" Petrosky, [1985]. Robert N. Endorser [1972] says that sports Psychology clarifies one's conduct in games and sports.

A verifiable glance at the field uncovered that like the beginning of numerous other conduct sciences, the underlying foundations of scientific investigation of psychology of sports follow back to the turn of the 20th century. In 1989, Triplett distributed the principal scientific investigation of sports psychology, announcing proof that "the substantial presence of another hopeful partaking at the same time in the race serves to free energy not usually accessible". This and other land mark concentrates anyway didn't prompt a more orderly investigation of the psychology of sports until Colemar R Griffith an instructive Psychologist of games and training in the last part of the 1920s. In spite of the fact that Griffith's scientific gainful' was colossal, the psychology of training and psychology and games were his essential commitment to the investigation of psychology of sports. Griffith proposed the standards of effective training on different subjects, shockingly Griffith's work on the psychology of sports reach a conclusion with the discontinuance of the athletic examination research center at the University of Illinois in 1932.

Albeit the underlying game psychology program at the University of Illinois was fleeting, the Soviet program filled in as model for other comparative program that later arisen in Eastern Europe and in the People's Republic of China. These projects zeroed in on the immediate utilization of information about psychology to sports and athletes, instead of on the revelation of the hypothetical facts.

In 1965, sport psychology overall was animated by the principal global congress of game psychology in Rome. This congress not just improved worldwide co-activity and correspondence. It likewise energized the development of public associations of those intrigued by the psychological consequences of game. By the 1980s such public social orders had been begun in numerous nations, and ensuing worldwide congress further sustains those rehearsing some type of sports psychology. Alongside the arrangement of National social orders there has been a multiplication of distributions dedicated to brandish psychology, including diary of game psychology [1970], The diary of applied game psychology, and diary of game conduct.

In spite of the fact that its substance regions started with a conduct accentuation, sport psychology is currently taking a gander at dynamic and global variables, with a significant interest in intervening variables, the competitor's insights and discernment.

Athletics

Competition in running, hopping or tossing normally goes once again into pre-history. The soonest proof we have of coordinated running is from around 3800 B.C. in Egypt and athletic accomplishments were especially valued at the old Olympic game in Greece. Those games were something beyond brandishing challenge for they were additionally incredible imaginative and social celebrations keeping up the Greek ideal of flawlessness of brain and body. They gave the motivation to the advanced Olympic games, which have given the concentration to athletics since their re-presentation in 1896. At any rate as of not long ago, separate big showdown for all occasions were organized in 1983, and now-a-days, there is a plenty of top Class competitions.

The principal public title were those of England in 1866, coordinated by the armature athletic club. These went before the arrangement of the Armature Athletic Association in 1880.

The world's first athletic club the Necton Guild was set up in Nafolk in 1817 by then ordinary competition was going on. In athletics there are two kinds of occasions.

1.   Track occasions it incorporates short, long, center distance races.

2.   Field levels it incorporates tossing and bouncing occasions. Olympic style events occasion is the primary game presented in Olympic.

Aggression

Aggression has been an expert subject in the examination of connections of people in the given social setting. Since aggression produces more sensational vicious types of conduct, numerous analysts think about it as a critical factor in examining relational connections. Numerous clarifications about the human savagery imply that aggression stems fundamentally from inborn inclinations and remotely evoked drives to hurt and harm others. Additionally, existing social conditions combined with past learning may likewise decide the amont of aggression an individual has.

Aggressiveness is all around found among all people. In a humanized and co-usable living, there is little spot for direct articulation of aggression.

Despite the fact that hidden or weakened types of aggressiveness are less problematic, even such conduct can be upsetting to acceptable relational connection. As Green and O'Neal (1976) call attention to dissatisfaction, actual assault, verbal badgering and affront are normal. In an advanced serious society disappointment gets a typical spot. Individuals are frequently unfit to manage the genuine wellspring of disappointment, which brings about serious passionate annoyed and maladaptive conduct.

Aggression is more probable when disappointment is seen as ridiculous, and it may not happen if the impeding of thought processes is thought of and advocated by the dissatisfaction doesn't really bring about aggression yet makes a status to act forcefully.

Aggression is a deliberate conduct coordinated towards an individual with an expectation to hurt. As Sigmund Frued (1920) estimated human aggression springs from the energy of crude passing inclination diverted towards others. Aggression is supposed to be instinctual and if not released, it develops until it detonates. Albeit the human inclination to aggress may not qualify as a nature, aggression is organically affected. In the event that naturally decided, the articulation, of aggression is identified with the level of specific chemicals (Testosterone) and an additional Y chromosome (XYY) in guys (Moyer, 1976, Svare, 1983). Gangs I an additional Y chromosome relates aggression to genetics.

The most well-known each day wellspring of aggression is verbal in pessimistic assessment from someone else (Boss, 1961). High temperature (Baron 1975) may likewise build aggression. Dismissed youngsters (Bousha and Twentymen, 1984), manhandled kids (Green, 1983), and genuinely attacked kids (George and Main, 1979) are more inclined to aggressiveness Some people are more forceful than others might be clarified regarding volatile contrast and support design the kid has encountered. Aggression in the event that it stem» from worked in inclinations or propensities, it can presumably never be dispensed with. It tends to be expanded because of ecological or situational impact.

The plenty of definitions given uncovers that aggression is a typical conduct of people and is considered as a guard component. In sports occasions, the forceful player should be guarded which pulls him toward the accomplishment of the game. All the while, the player utilizes all the sports abilities in guarding the group and brings achievement.

Self Concept (SC) in Sports

Self concept is most affecting factor on singular conduct. It has cozy relationship with individual parts of people, which decide the scholastic, sports, and different circles of the person. Self concept is imagined as an arrangement of mentality towards one self. Because of involvement an individual structures mentalities that puts together into a self steady framework to shield against dangers and assaults. In this manner it comprises of all the abrupt of sentiments, mentalities, yearnings, needs, estimations of one-self, concerning one self. In this way self concept is simply the picture of one that is particular from another. It fuses his view of what he is truly loved and of his work as an individual just as his motivations for development achievement. This self concept is viewed as a self-supporter in some random errand. The higher individual picture has constructive outcomes. It is normal that an individual with positive £ mythical being respect accomplishes better. Essentially a sports execution can be upgraded by building up a positive self concept in the athletes. Subsequently self concept is a factor that is accepted to influence the exhibition of sportsman decidedly.

CHAPTER-II

CONCEPTUAL FRAME WORK

Aggression

Aggression is a deliberate behavior towards an individual with a reason to make harm that individual. It is the character quality which can be comprehensively characterized as a structure to behavior, including endeavors to dominate an undertaking and the term aggression is for the most part used to apply to activity with expectation to harm others. The recurrence of more strange types of maladaptive aggression is presumably identified with the way that aggression is close to sex-the profoundly controlled and quelled of a wide range of human's social behavior. Forceful behavior and its causes along these lines have extraordinary importance for social researchers. What's more, disappointment is one of the reasons for forceful behavior.

All dissatisfaction makes aggression. Disappointment is the aftereffect of some power meddling with the advancement towards an objective. The ordinary method of managing disappointment is to distant the obstacle repressing with the advancement. However, under particular conditions this regular method of managing hindrances is denied. Subsequently dissatisfaction is transformed into a free-coasting aggression. In the modem serious society disappointments are normal and individuals can't battle the genuine wellsprings of these dissatisfactions. Subsequently there is a free-skimming aggression whose advantageous targets are the individuals from the out-gathering. On being hindered while seeking after an objective, an individual is baffled which brings about the excitement of forceful drive. Be that as it may, if the wellspring of dissatisfaction is either not inside his range or inaccessible, the people feel denied and this hardship may bring about forceful propensities (Berkowtiz, 1969). As Moyer (1976) puts dissatisfaction by and large prompts aggression; however some different conditions have additionally been found to build the forceful potential.

At the point when an individual endures serious or delayed disappointment, his powerlessness to accomplish an objective may offer ascent to sensations of individual disappointment and uneasiness The gathered pressure emerging out of industrious dissatisfaction frequently discovers articulation in forceful demonstrations. Aggressiveness may make the types of emotions and moves of outrage and wrath, of real physical viciousness against articles and individuals and of verbal assault, of dreams of brutality and assault. Under certain conditions, the aggression may even be turned internal against the self.

Aggression is typically characterized as physical or verbal behavior coordinated toward an individual or article with a reason to cause harm on that individual or item. In depicting instinctual behavior, Sigmund Freud (1920) clarified aggression as the cognizant sign and projection of the demise senses or thanatos. As Murray (1938) calls attention to, aggression is the need to attack, or harm others, to disparage, damage, scorn or denounce malignantly, to rebuff harshly or to participate in cruel practices. Taking into account Harry Kaufmann (1970) aggression is one that incorporates behavior that is guided against another people to communicate the expectation or want to perpetrate injury.

Arnold Buss 1961) in his audit of hypothesis and examination on aggression characterizes aggression is a reaction that conveys poisonous boosts to another living being. Development against others is by and large debilitate to individuals from social framework except if it is coordinated against wellsprings of danger. Such a behavior is ordinarily depicted as hostile and aggression. The term 'hostile' is utilized to portray the attitudinal foundation of the behavior, where as the term 'aggressive' generally alludes to the demonstration of moving against someone else.

Buss (1961) grouped aggression into dynamic versus inactive, direct versus aberrant and physical versus verbal. It is accepted that a both inactive and roundabout aggression, it is hard to distinguish that assailant, who in this manner is probably not going to endure counter aggression. The more outlandish the counter aggression, the more plausible the aggression. Besides, disappointment is a critical factor in deciding the degree of aggression. It is important in this way, that disappointment ought to evoke more regular and exceptional, aggression, when the admissible aggression is detached and aberrant that when it is dynamic and direct. The distinction among dynamic and uninvolved aggression is that in dynamic aggression an individual communicates his activities that are observable, while in inactive aggression he doesn't show his aggressive activities through there is aggression in him. Direct aggression implies eye to eye contact with individual being assaulted, while circuitous aggression happens without such contacts. Further the physical and verbal aggression alludes to substantial damage and assault with words separately. In grown-ups, verbal aggression is more incessant than physical aggression that is hindered during the interaction of socialization. In view of this hindrance, disappointment is less inclined to prompt aggression when the passable aggression is physical then when it is verbal.

Aggression is additionally named instrumental (Buss, 1966) and hostile aggression (Baron, 1977). In instrumental aggression the individual uses aggression as a method of fulfilling some intention.

Hostile aggression is any type of behavior coordinated toward to objective of hurting or harming another person.

Different researchers have offered a few hypotheses of aggression. The most conspicuous hypothesis is the disappointment - aggression hypothesis created by Dollard and others (1939). As indicated by this hypothesis dissatisfaction consistently prompts some type of aggression. When there is impedance in arriving at an objective there is disappointment, which prompts aggressive behavior. Buss (1966) brings up that this hypothesis stresses that aggression happens just in presence of outrage and disregards an entire class of aggressive reactions. As per Leonard Berkowitz (1965) dissatisfaction - aggression speculation ought to be changed threely: First, the feeling that outcomes from disappointments (Anger) doesn't really bring about aggression, yet makes just a status for aggressively, aggression won't happen except if there are appropriate signs accessible. Third, rather than proposing that all aggression is because of disappointment, it is currently realized that suitable prompts may prompt aggressive behavior Therefore aggressive propensities can be adapted only by noticing the signs without the student essentially being baffled. In this manner the disappointment aggression speculation as expressed by Dollard and others have been censured, as all aggression isn't the result of dissatisfaction. Individuals aggression for a wide range of reasons and in light of various factors, for example, boxes hit and harm not on the grounds that they are disappointed however it is there job to do as such. Just when disappointment is solid, and just when it is seen as discretionary of ill-conceived, it will in general improve the probability of aggression, when it is frail, or saw as merited and genuine, it seems to have little effect upon resulting aggression (Kulik and Brown, 1979; Worchele, 1974). Henceforth dissatisfaction s just one of numerous factors adding to human aggression.

The old style torment hypothesis of aggression previously began with crafted by Pavlov (1963). Torments vary in kind and degree starting with one individual then onto the next and starting with one time then onto the next in a similar individual. The part of agony evoking human aggression can be perceived by the power of difficult prompts related with the assailant, which may prompt aggressive behavior. Subsequently dread of torment is traditionally molded and frequently prompts incredibly aggressive behavior. To carry on more aggressively is to limit the agony experienced by the person. Subsequently the experience of torment will make the individual more aggressive.

The intuition hypothesis recommends that individuals some way or another customized for aggressive behavior. Sigmund Freud (1920), an eminent Psychoanalyst who contributed altogether in the advancement of impulse hypothesis, in the clarification of aggressive behavior of people, completely articulated that the human aggression has a base in his natural inclinations. Clearly the intuition hypothesis holds that the people are aggressive due to their instinctual characteristics. Freud firmly accepted that aggression originates from an amazing passing intuition controlled by every individual and consequently the impulse is at first meant to self annihilation, which is accordingly, diverted outward towards others with a goal of hurting them. In this way the vast majority of individuals are driven by their senses to be aggressive as hypothesis clarifies. Anyway there can be variety n the statement of aggressive demonstrations relying on the measure of existing inborn aggressive affinity. One powerful thought regarding human aggression is that piece of "the idea of the monster" (Freud, 1920; Lorenz, 1966). Individuals are said to impart an aggressive impulse to bring down creatures and human aggression is supposed to be an animal groups normal behavior. It is accounted for that bits of human and lower creature cerebrum control the outflow of aggression and that levels of specific chemicals (testosterone) are identified with aggression (Moyer, 1976; Svare, 1983). Dismissing 'human instinct' perspective on aggression, a few clinicians stress the significance of ecological, social and learning factors in the causation and guideline of aggressive behavior (Bandura, 1983; Baron, 1977; Berkovvitz, 1962). As indicated by Orthogenic perspective, essential drives are positive and 'ha: organic entities will create in sound and positive manners, except if kept from doing as such by a few ecological stress (Roger, 1951; Combs and Snygg, 1959).

Aggression isn't an interaction that rises out of a circumstance yet rather exists like repositories of characterized sum, inside every person, to be turned on or off. To be aggressive is the power of qualities. Hence aggression is hereditarily decided, as sociobiology claims. Further it is guaranteed that qualities don't itself code the characteristic however potential is surrendered and the attribute possibly emerges when the proper natural prompt is given. Along these lines Socio-researcher stress that the human aggressive behavior is an underlying, unsurprising example of collaboration among qualities and climate.

Jacobs, Brunton and Melville (1965) proposed that 47 XYY disorder a chromosomal irregularity was significantly more hall among people detained for savage wrongdoings than among the populace on the loose. Ownership of an extra 'Y' chromosome joins genetics and aggression, Jarvik et.al. (1973) and Lloyd and Weiz (1975) recommended that the disorder embroils the single 'Y' chromosome controlled by ordinary guys is liable for sex distinction in aggression.

Social learning hypothesis accentuates the way that aggression ought to be seen essentially as a learned type of social behavior. Allies of this view (Bandura, 1983; Baron, 1977; Berkowitz, 1983) contend that people are nor brought into the world with a huge cluster of aggressive reactions available to them; rather the should get familiar with these behavior similarly as they learn other complex types of behavior. Impersonation of others' behavior is one of the reasons for aggression Modeling is another reason, which is more powerful as it guides the spectators focus toward one of the conceivable behavior successions, show the onlooker that specific behaviors are OK and upgrade the enthusiastic excitement of the eyewitness which, under certain conditions, can encourage aggression and show the spectator some particular aggressive activities that might be replicated. Hence the social learning hypothesis underscores the job of learning in acting aggressively either through impersonation or model in Classical molding and instrumental condition kg are similarly other significant wellsprings of human aggression. As of now clarified old style molding happens when certain upgrades or circumstances are matched with one another. Through speculation, the aggressive behavior may spread until the individual acts in an aggressive manner toward numerous comparative upgrades. On the other, instrumental molding of aggression happens when individuals are compensated, or built up for their aggressive behavior. As indicated by the standards of instrumental molding, behaviors which are built up are bound to happen later on. Hence, if aggression is built up it might turn into a constant reaction by and large.

On the off chance that human aggression has its base in learning a particular natural and social factors, it can likewise be decreased and controlled, in the premium or keeping away from any negative and destructive outcomes. Discipline for aggression has been one of the old style ways to deal with the control of human aggression. Discipline is compelling when it is solid and promptly follows the aggressive behavior When discipline isn't viable, it might increment aggressive inclinations, as discipline is a frustrator, and may excite and outrage the individual being rebuffed.

Another way to deal with the decrease of outrage and aggression is therapy. Therapy alludes to venting a feeling, or "getting it out of one's framework". While therapy may help diminished indignation for a brief timeframe, it doesn't appear to diminish the probability that will aggress later on against a specific individual who drove one mad. On the off chance that therapy happens an individual should feel much improved and be less aggressive. Two sorts of emotive delivery appear to happen in individuals; verbalized therapy and development therapy. In the sense, the therapy accepts a job of pressure decreasing capacity. Another way to deal with the control of aggression depends on the idea that specific feelings and sentiments are inconsistent with outrage and aggression (Baron, 1977). Henceforth, aggression whether grew socially or organically should be tended to as the improvement of character antagonistically gets affected.

In spite of the accentuation on aggression as a learned behavior, there is an extensive help for the possibility that aggression is an inalienable trademark. Sex contrasts in aggressive reacting are likewise generally acknowledged thought. Many examination discoveries show that aggressiveness will in general be an ordinary male trademark. Guys of some random species are more aggressive than females (Scott, 1958). Terman and Tyler (1954) have gathered a lot of proof con r sex contrasts identified with aggressiveness. Explores on creatures; (Collias youngsters (Feshbach, 1980; Lansky et.al (1961) and grown-ups (Buss, 1963: Prasad, 1980) propose sexual dimorphism in aggression. Ladies are really the delicate sex generally liberated from aggressive urges (Baron and Byrne, 1981). Yet, lately orderly exploration on this issue proposes that ladies are less aggressive than men just under specific conditions, particularly when ladies accept that such behavior is improper and conflicting with ladylike sex jobs. In circumstances where such limitations are missing, distinction between the genders may diminish or even thoroughly disappear (Fordi, Macaualay and Thorne, 1977). Obvious proof for this view is given by z n try directed by Richardson, Bernstein and tailor (1979), which proposes that the generally low degree of aggression frequently appeared by females originates from their conviction that such behavior will be seen is sex unseemly by others. Conditions serving 10 eliminate such limit; nay empower higher le/els of aggression. Maccoby and Jackline, (1974 s have inferred that there is a significant organic reason for the distinction in aggression, as it is identified with the degrees of chemicals (Maccoby and Jack 1974) and the social impact (Tieger, 1980) which influence the degree of aggression in people. Both natural and ecological impacts play a significant job in the pace of aggression. Guys are more aggressive than female. A distinction that shows up at an early age and proceeds into adulthood where communicated as inclination to overwhelm. Hence there is sex contrast in aggressive behavior.

The most normally regular wellspring of aggression is a verbal affront or antagonistic assessment from someone else (Buss, 1961). Unsavory and aversive natural conditions may arrange a few group toward aggression High temperature (Baron, 1977), exceptional commotion (Donnesstien and Welson, 1976), and swarming (Freedman 1975) are found to build aggression particularly in individuals who have effectively been incensed somehow or another. It is discovered that ignored (Bousha and Twentymen, 1S84), mishandled (Wasserman, Green and Allen, 198j) and physically attacked children (George and Main, 1979) exhibit high paces of physical aggression. Bandura and Walters (1963) call attention to that subject can secure aggressive propensities only by noticing the behavior of aggressive model-guardians being the models. As indicated by Sears, Maccoby and Levin (1957) guardians who impressively utilize physical discipline have children who are more aggressive. In the event that parent:; become more hostile and utilize more physical discipline and need warmth and love in managing their children, they become more aggressive (Patterson, 1976).

In youth, children face a significant new undertaking; learn n to communicate terrible sentiments that are vented as aggressive behavior in socially adequate manners. The facts confirm that aggressive behavior especially physical" aggression is more normal in early years. As kid achieves higher age levels the verbal abilities improve and there is move toward more prominent utilization of verbal aggression, for example, provoking and ridiculing. Bandura et. Al. (1963) expressed that the particular type of aggression that children pick may have a lot to do with what they have realized regularly through perception. Direct support or prize may cultivate aggressive behavior. Limit of aggressive models through vicarious learning is likely, particularly in the light of proof that small kids go to inconsistently to TV and may not comprehend the connections between aggressive activities and any discipline depicted (Collins, 1983). In this manner aggression may likewise be encouraged through TV and movies which greaterly affect the children.

Importance of Aggression in Sport :

The type of aggression saw in game might be arranged in to (1) competitor's and (2) onlooker's aggression or antagonism. The serious idea of game, maybe, is the significant purpose behind the athletes carrying on aggressively particularly in physical games where the intuitive inclinations of offense and protection (crude or racial types of behavior focusing on battle for presence and natural selection) are straightforwardly reflected in the abilities and activities of the members. The stray for matchless quality, strength and greatness clearly includes a wide range of aggression-retaliatory, instrumental, direct circuitous, and so forth Aggression in one from or the other is unavoidable and certain in donning action.

What precisely triggers off aggression particularly retaliatory aggression in athletes, can't be handily clarified in light of the fact that the hypothetical perspectives on this issue are dissimilar. In any case, different examination contemplates led in this space show that the factors prompting aggression in athletes might be outside (natural, situational) or inside (persuasive drives) or both. Cox (1995) has recorded a few factors related with the event of aggression in sports explicit setting. The rundown incorporates: (1) ecological temperature, (2) impression of adversaries goals to concurs (the competitor who sees that an adversary is attempting to cause mischief will react similarly), (3) dread of counter (a survivor of aggression will fight back significantly more aggressively), and (4) design of the game nearer the physical contact between the rivals, the more prominent the possibility for fight back: for retaliatory aggression). Game variables which frequently lead to aggressive behavior are summed up as (a) point differential (closer the score of the rival groups, the lesser the possibility of aggression; in a particularly basic game circumstance, where punishments for aggression are serious, players and mentors don't face challenge of being aggressive); (b) playing at home or away (every cockerel battles best on his own dunghill, or it very well might be in any case additionally) (c) result of interest (rout in an installation causes athletes to act all the more aggressively towards themselves, authorities, mentors), (d) association standings (the lower the standing or rating of a group, the more aggressive it is in its battle to improve its standing) and (e) times of play (Aggression increments as the game continues, the time of play and force of aggression are discovered related).

There is sufficient proof such that athletics partaking in physical games like boxing, wrestling, judo and so forth are more aggressive than those taking an interest in non-physical games. A few therapists are persuaded that aggression in certain facilitates is unborn, others trust it is obtained as a spirit legacy. It is hard to say whether inherently aggressive people take to aggressive sports or athletes become aggressive by cooperation in sports including inordinate aggression. Verbose exploration contemplates neither affirm this nor refute it. Maybe, longitudinal investigations may tackle this question in future.

High actuation in players and observers is additionally supposed to be one reasons of aggression in sorts. High excitement (initiation) catalyzes more energetic exertion and activity because of which individuals become more aggressive to accomplish their destinations. In this cycle, regardless of whether they mean to curve any mischief on the adversary is no easy to refute, the essential issue is that over-initiation with such communication normally prompts a type of aggression. Cratty (1989) appropriately brings up, enactment, along with the incitement of a clearly purposefully aggressive demonstration by a person who might be effectively fought back against, will commonly trigger direct aggression. This especially is valid, if the attacker isn't probably going to languish any authorizations over the aggression and if the casualty has, before, been remunerated and seen the utility of direct close to home aggression ("battling dominates games"). However, actuation itself is emphatically not a legitimate explanation the aggression to happen, some natural factors should exist to arouse it. So enactment may not reason aggression in sports. Related to some situational factor, it might help spread it.

Aggression in some structure penetrates the athletic scene. Its partners show up in athletes at moderately youthful age. The soul of competition and the desire to dominate, rule or quell the rival start to win and keep on supporting all through athletes vocation when they come to understand the "contending energetically" both physically and psychologically, is an endorsed from of serious behavior. That, maybe, is the reasons why a few athletes move admissible constraints of aggressive behavior (particularly retaliatory aggression). This separated, Bandura (1973) obviously explained that athletes enjoy aggressive demonstrations of behavior since they are valued, granted or compensated either in unmistakable ways like winning or getting cash that occasionally goes with athletic achievement, or through acquiring status and different types of social prizes. Indeed, even emotions and slants communicated by the well wishers, onlookers or fans appreciating aggressiveness are adequately satisfactory to affect further aggression and set future patterns.

Sports competition without "aggression" is a body without soul. Competition and aggression are twins. There is obvious proof that, as a rule, aggression in more rambunctious games, may help execution since it stirs players overlay to invest more enthusiastically exertion, and do and pass on for the achievement of the group. Oppositely, there is likewise sign, that aggression submitted by players in specific settings, circumstances or positions may block execution of individual ability just as achievement of the group. This dumbfounding perspective might be ascribed to contrasts in people and game circumstances. The force of aggression showed by players in a game or a specific match may enormously rely upon the common conditions and ground real factors i.e., similar people carrying on substantially more aggressively in one circumstance yet not in other. The temperament (mental air or condition of body and brain) of the players - regardless of whether they are winning or losing-is likewise a significant thought in the amount and nature of aggression communicated. As Cratty (1989) suitably brings up, aggression that a competitor may concede to encounter, might be affected by blend of factors, including job insights, the way wherein aggression connects with expertise, and the legends encompassing the game.

Significance of Self concept (SC)

Self concept has been alluded to as one's disposition towards oneself (Love, 1961). It is a coordinated arrangement of discernments, accepts, feedings, mentalities, and qualities which the individual perspectives as a piece of attributes himself (Paderson, 1965). Rogers (1951) characterized self concept as a coordinated arrangements of impression of the self which are acceptable to mindfulness It is made out of such components as the view of one's attributes and exercises; the percepts and concepts of the self corresponding to other people and to the climate, the worth characteristics which are seen as partner, encounters and protests, and the objectives goals which are seen as sure or antagonistic valence. Saraswat and Gaur (1931) portrayed self concepts as the self concept is simply the people method of looking. It additionally means the perspective of feeling and carrying on. There are a few terms that are essentially inseparable from self concept, among there are, self picture, the personality, self agreement, self discernment and incredible self.

In late socio-psychological investigations of character, self-hypothesis is a significant one. It basically comprises of self-assessment and private encounters. Self is converted right into it by the mentalities we have, by the convictions wt hold. Self concept in wide terms alludes to an individual's impression of himself or herself (Shavellon et al, 1976). These discernments are shaped generally through inductions drawn from encounters and rewards and discipline further impact them. Impression of self impacts activities, which, thusly, influence the manners by which the self is seen. A comprehension of an individual's self-concept gives a premise to clarifying and foreseeing how that individual will act (Sharielson et al 1976).

Self concept is key to human character. It is the pinnacle and is the perfection of all friendly and individual encounters that we have had (Sullivon 1947, 1953). As indicated by Shaelson et al, (1976), the constituents of self-concept are:

1) It being structured and organized

2) Multifacted, for example a few unique classes might be shaped, viz, school, work place, social acknowledgment, physical engaging quality, buddy gathering, scholarly capacity and

3) The clear cut design of self-concept can be portrayed progressively on an element of consensus.

Self concept might be considered as a bunch of assumptions in addition to assessment of the territories or behavior concerning which those hopes curve held (Mccomdliss, 1961). Self-concept is something perplexing, it is an element of the prize and qualities in its different aspects and offers ascend to good or negative feelings.

As indicated by Cooley (1902), "Self is a social item that arises as the child associates with others". Self has essentially three components.

a)   Once creative mind of the manner in which we appear to other people

b)   One view of the way other present their appearance; and

c)   The way we feel about those decisions.

Cooley (1902) believed that people self-picture and self-regard rely vigorously upon the criticism he/she got as a child, an understudy, a specialist, a dad, etc. As per him without a social novel, there can never be an ability to be self aware.

As indicated by Mead (1934), social behavior is a predecessor to self. He stressed the significance of social life and abstract insight. He clarifies any behavior regarding social behaviorism, which imply that the view of self relies on the reaction of others. It is just when we consider different people groups perspectives on us that we get a picture of ourselves. He expresses that the individual has a 'self which is an excellent determinant of behavior, just comparable to the selves of different individuals from his social gathering. The construction of his self mirrors his overall behavior example of the social gathering to which he has a place. Indeed, even o her individual having a place o this gathering will have the self with comparative construction the entire connection example of coordinated social behavior which that society or local area shows or is continuing and its coordinated design is established by this example (Mean, 1934, P. 202). The coordinated local area or social gathering which provides for the individual is solidarity of self which might be known as the summed up other (Mead, 1934, P. 154). The mentalities of the summed up other are the perspectives of the entire local area. It is this type of summed up other that impact the behavior of the individual engaged with social cycles. All locally practices authority over the direct of its individuals. It is in this structure that the social cycle or local area enters as a deciding factor into the people's reasoning (Mead, 1934, P. 154)

As indicated by Coleman (1969), 'self-concept' is an image or picture of himself, his perspective on himself as particular from different things and people. The self-picture fuses howdy; view of what he is truly similar to (self-personality) and of his work personally (self-assessment) just as his goals for development and achievement (self-ideal).

Jersild (1963) states: "The self, as it at last develops in a composite of considerations and feelings, which comprise an individual consciousness of his individual presences, his impression of what he has, his conception of what he is, and his feelings about this attributes, characteristics and viewpoints". Secord and Backman (1964) characterize self as "Every single one of us has a bunch of perceptions and feelings towards ourselves".

As Maslow (1954), puts it, realizing self is "non extreme need, sufficiency, his main impetus for the craving to upgrade himself inside wonder field; which he calls self-realization. The self develops into adulthood orally halfway by level headed or emotional revelation, uncovering and tolerating what is inward nature of that individual.

Rogers, (1951) characterizes that harmonious self is the "Coordinated, reliable conceptual gestalt, made out of view of the qualities of 'I' or ' me' to other and the different parts of coexistence with the qualities appended so these discernments.

As per Mc David and Harari, (1968), the term 'self-concept' is utilized to allude to the coordinated intellectual design got from one's encounters of his own self. It was perceived that an individual may show certain misperception and twisting in his comprehension of himself, similarly as he may misperceive or contort, his view of others. For this very explanation the term self-concept was advanced.

Obviously from the above expressed definitions and hypothetical depiction that the self (and self concept) is the superb determinant of character and behavior. The improvement of self is controlled by the behavior of the others who are important to him.

Apparently an individual isn't brought into the world with a self concept. It is shaped is a consequence of one's experience and response to the climate. As child develops he learns about his encompassing as well as about himself. As Hall and Lindzey (1957) put it self concept alludes to an individual's mentality and feeling about himself.

Guilford (1966) views self as concept as an individual insight,' disposition and feelings about himself. Albeit self-concept is exceptionally perplexing, the greater part of the scientists done to-date primarily identifies with the two elements of self-concept (a) positive, negative self concept and (b) saw self-concept.

A few researches have illuminated these elements of self concept. Oliver (1975) accepts that the achievement builds up the positives self concept. Riley (1933) examined between connection between self-concept and physical execution. Ice (1970) inferred that all sportsmen are of the assessment that "other's insight", fills in as an additional and significant upgrade to perform well, move them to invest more effort and inspire to perform better. Catch and Johnson (1954, 1967), Brunner (1969), Reid and Hey (1979), Schendel (1965, 1970), additionally discovered athletes to have high feeling of individual work and high self concept. In the field of sports, self-concept is considered as perhaps the most valuable apparatuses to get, guide and teach the sportsman.

Concept of performance

The nature of sports performance has been deficiently investigated on the grounds that sports execution is a muddled multi-dimensional interaction of handling a sports task. Its investigation further requirements an incorporated exertion with respect to different training science orders and hypothesis and techniques for explicit sports. Human development, human execution is a subject for such shifted sciences as exercise, physiology neuro-physiology, bio-mechanics, psychology, human artificial intelligence and so forth (Brook and Whiting, 1975.

The performance of sports is a cycle of handling a given motor task. The degree, to which this errand has been satisfied, is the aftereffect of the way toward handling the engine task. Accordingly, the concept of sports execution ought to incorporate the genuine interaction of handling the undertaking.

The sports performance is characterized as, "solidarity of execution and aftereffect of sports activity or an unpredictable grouping of sports activities estimated or assessed by concurred and socially decided names" (Schnable, 1987).

The real exhibition is the psycho-socio-organic cycle. The idea of sports execution can be seen totally simply by considering this cycle. The investigation of this cycle will handle variable data about the construction of execution accordingly giving important data having suggestions about training. Along these lines it is of most extreme significance to comprehend the sports performance as a solidarity of development and its outcome.

Schnable (1981) has built up the concept of sports execution and if s different viewpoints. The sports execution is the consequence of the deciphered activity of different control and administrative cycle, occurring at different levels of the focal sensory system and awareness. These cycles decide the engine co-appointment and discover articulation in the development structure and in characteristics and attributes of sports development.

The overall presentation design of sports exercises can be addressed as a model, which is an exceptionally improved on representation of the genuine exhibition structure. Cratty (1987), Gundlach (1967), Letzeller (1979) have attempted to delineate the exhibition factors conveyed in bunches at different levels, each more significant level comprising of factors which are more explicit for execution when contrasted with those of the lower level. A particularly model does exclude a few factors (eg. Outside factors) which impact the exhibition during the focal competition. Verchosankij (1971), then again, received a one of a kind methodology by introducing the exhibition of triple hop as the relationship existing between Hop Step and Jump and execution in other related exercises. Such methodology, be that as it may, doesn't illuminate predominance and interrelationships among factors like, procedure, strategies, restrictive and coordinative capacities and psychological factors. An ideal model of execution structure, which can address the sports execution, has natural, psychological, neuro-physiological and robotic perspectives, which cannot all be represented n a solitary model.

The structure of sports performance should portray the accompanying:

a)   The interaction of performance

b)   Factors deciding factors

c)   The relative strength/weightage of these factors

d)   The between relationship existing among the factors.

A model of design or structure of the sports performance dependent on Schnable's concept alerts as under:

1.   It is an overall model of sports performance and not of performance in a specific sports.

2.   The structure of performance of every sportsman will contrast from that of all other sportsmans.

The model of sports performance comprises of two things: design of the cycle of performance and the construction of performance limit, which offers ascend to sports performance.

1.   Structure of the Process of Performance

It is the structure or design of the genuine cycle of performing. At the end of the day, it is the physical, physiological, mechanical physic of the engine activity or activities done during the competition. Engine activities comprise of developments, which are controlled and managed by the focal sensory system. Contingent upon the idea of sports subjective and subjective estimations of various chose boundaries \i his multi-dimensional cycle are recorded or estimated to find out about this interaction.

2.	Structure of the Performance Capacity

The performance limit alongside outer factors decides the sports performance. Performance limit is an unpredictable performance, which is partitioned into five gatherings.

1. personality: It comprises of conviction, values, interest, perspectives, disposition, intellectual abilities, character characteristics, propensities and so forth.

2. Condition: it is otherwise called physical wellness. It comprises of solidarity, speed, perseverance and their intricate structures.

3. Technique/Co-appointment: it comprises of technical skills, adaptability and coordinative capacities.

4. Tactics: It comprises of tactical knowledge, tactical skill and tactical abilities.

5. Constitution: It is comprises of constitution, body tallness and weight, size, width and length of body parts, muscle to fat ratio, slender weight and steadiness of bones, joints and so forth

All these five factors are between related and between subordinate. The level of significance of these factors for performance is extraordinary and henceforth training for each sport should be contrastingly formed guarantee the ideal advancement of every performance factor for better and higher sports performance. Like the construction of competition performance, the distinctive performance essentials are the outcome and articulation of co-appointment and lively cycle of the human framework. Subsequently, for additional investigation of every performance pre-imperative an incorporated exertion on the pieces of different human sciences is fundamental.

The model of performance structure is an errand of hypothesis and technique for each sport to set up a model of performance construction of its own action. In explicit sports a particularly model cm e further separated in its sub-segments. Bauersfled and Schroter (1979) have introduced such models for each order of Track and Field sport. The model of performance structure in explicit sports arrangement has two significant capacities:

a. It empowers one to comprehend the beginning of sports performance in a given sport based on which the guidelines for training at different stages and periods can be sensibly determined.

b. It helps sporting talent among young sportsmen for supplier sport (Schlibe, 1980). On the off chance that we know the important performance essentials for great performance in a sport and their relative significance, we can choose those sportsmen who have the capability of accomplishing an undeniable level in those prerequisites at a later stages.

Each model of performance structure represents the summed up injury of performance of the top class sportsman. Consequently the sportsmen have various degrees of different performance pre-essentials. Thusly, as a general rule, the design of performance of every sportsman will contrast from that of other sportsman For instance, two hurlers may give a similar performance (eg. 21.50 m in shotput), yet one may be contingent more on strength and speed to accomplish this performance though the other, ailing in these two capacities, accomplishes tin same performance based on his better method. Additionally, the performance design of sportsmen and children will be unique.

The sports performance in global competitions and competitions (i.e., elite) not just signify the undeniable degree of psychomotor limit of an in dissenter sportsman yet in addition gives articulation of the record and proficient country and society Kunath (1968). The social conditions, which are fundamental for delivering title holders, fill in as an important medium wherein the ability choice, sports, training and sports competitions can be done successfully. Without this supporting medium, sports can't create to significant level. Title holders created by German Democratic Republic and Russian are not just the result of their mentors, teachers and families, yet additionally of the social orders, societies and political frameworks to which they have a place.

CHAPTER-III

REVIEW OF LITERATURE

Sports psychology is a relatively new field of research. In this chapter some of the variable studied in relation to sports persons and their performance are given briefly.

Self Concept and Sports Performance

Self concept is perhaps the most overwhelming factors affecting the individual behavior. It is initially was considered to the cornerstone particle mandate guiding by Rogers, is presently taken as critical in the field of sports, training and so forth It has close associations for certain close to home angles like inclining, inspiration, perspectives, insight and change which decide the scholarly, sports and different triumphs of the person.

Self concept is best considered as an arrangement of perspectives towards one self. Similarly as an individual because of encounters, structures disposition which coordinates into a self steady framework and protects against dangers and assaults. So the individual additionally shapes perspectives towards himself. Self-concept comprises of the multitude of discernments, feelings, perspectives, yearnings and estimations of one self concerning one self.

Apparently an individual isn't brought into the world with a self concept. It is framed because of one's experience and response to the climate. As child develops he learns about his encompassing as well as about himself. Lobby and Lindzey (1957) self concept alludes to an individual's demeanor and feeling about himself.

Guilford (1966) see self as concept as an individual discernment mentality and feelings about himself. Albeit self-concept is profoundly intricate the vast majority of the researches done to-date chiefly identifies with the two elements of self-concept (a) positive, negative sell concept and (b) saw self-concept.

A few researches have illuminated these components of self concept. Oliver (1975) accepts that the succers builds up the positive self concept.

Riley (1983) contemplated between connection between self-concept and physical performance. Ice (1970) inferred that all sportsmen are of the assessment that "others discernment". Fills in as an additional and significant improvement to perform rouse them to put in more effort and propel to perform better. Hutton and I (1954, 1967), Brunne (1969), Reid and Hey (1979), Schendel (1965, 1970).

Likewise, additionally discovered athletes to have high feeling of individual work and high self concept.

In the field of sports, self-concept is considered as quite possibly the most valuable instrument to get, float and teach the sportsman.

The self is a separated bit of the incredible field, comprising of cognizant and estimations of an I or me. The self concept is the focal image of what I am as an individual with a specific history and sets of yearnings. The individual responds in a coordinated entire to the exceptional field to fulfill the necessities, the most significant is simply the need to keep up and upgrade the self.

An investigation was directed by Shivaramakrishnan (1991) to analyze the degrees of sports accomplishments inspiration, self-concept, and attribute tension between Indian men b-ball and volleyball volley ball groups and Indian men b-ball and groups preceding their competition in the 1991 South Asian alliance games. 8 players in each gathering ball and volleyball were picked as subject for the examination. The examination uncovers that volleyball men shows preferred self-concept level over ball men and volleyball ladies players showed preferable self-concept over b-ball ladies cooperative people.

Kirchner (1978) self picture is quite possibly the most significant for entertainers in inclining engine expertise. He suggests that physical schooling exercises should be introduced so that each child makes some progress. As achievement in engine abilities rely on physical wellness, it ought to be proposed that physical wellness as reflected through fruitful mastering of an engine expertise would upgrade self-picture and consequently it could be theorized that there may be accordingly connection between's self-concept and physical wellness.

In a test study, Keffer (1978) directed Tennessee self-concept scale to gauge self-concept, and Coopers test to quantify cardiovascular wellness of young adult young men, results showed improvement in the self-concept and cardiovascular wellness after cooperation a running concept program. The high wellness bunch showed more certain self-relationship investigation of physical and psychological credits.

Graves (1974) discovered relationship of speed with physical self, social self and absolute character and strength with the physical self, while complete I-score of physical ascribes co related with physical self, social and all out character.

Donald and Ray (1973) revealed a positive huge connection between detailed interest in sports and self concept scores in the seventh, eighth and ninth grade young men yet not between physical capacity and self-concept.

Porat, Gershen (1989) psychological parts add to choose young female gymnasts. Chosen 20 young ladies (matured 7 to 9 years) for a 1 year study that surveyed the part of psychological variables (for example self concept, locus of control and tension) in serious tumbling. Subjects were regulate a the Tennessee self-concept scale', a locus of control scale for children and the state attribute tension scale following a time of training, to subjects partook in vaulting competitions. 10 psychological measures represented 49% of the performance change. The individual self-concept, trailed by locus of control, recognizes self-concept and attribute nervousness.

Forehand (1971) clarifies that self-concept has in direct experience shaped the comments Mid responses from others, correlations with what is perused or seen glancing in the mirror and reflection and conjecturers about the self gives materials to all these source particularly in childhood. As contrasted and childhood, in an assortment freedom to interface, with others in an assortment of social circumstance other than physical training are more, and he turns out to be more' reality arranged, the further advancement of self-concept by physical wellness alone is by all accounts rather restricted.

Werner (1972) is additionally of the view that despite the fact that psychology and psychiatry could help in the more certain territories of self-concept, drives, requirements and perspectives, great self-concept could be straightforwardly evolved through fruitful investment in games and sports exercises proper to sex job ID. Fiery physical schooling exercises reflecting physical wellness is generally related to the male sex, consequently, the connection between's physical wellness and self-concept ought to be more noteworthy in young men than in young ladies.

Stephen, Bailey and Werley (1990) led an examination on homeroom climate and locus of control in recognizing high and low self-concept in fourth and fifth graders. fourth and fifth graders finished the wharfs Hams children's self concept scale, the Nowicki-Strickland locus of control scale for children, and the study hall climate scale. Examination showed that 4 variables in mix (request end association, alliance, development, locus of control) effectively arranged 76% of all subjects recommending the significance of natural factors related with study hall and locus of control in recognizing self-concepts of children of primary young.

Salokun (1990) examined 112 high and low performance athletes in Nigeria and 108 non-athletes tall subjects mean age 16.8 years) who finished in Tennis self-concept scale. Athletes scored essentially higher on all self-concept sub-scales aside from behaviors, good, moral and family. Superior athletes scored fundamentally higher on all parts of self concept.

Robert, S. (1975) in exploring the self-impression of youth baseball players, announced that appraisals of exertion and capacity (interior factors) were higher in win than in misfortune conditions. Beforehand fruitless groups credited prompt accomplishment to shaky causes as did already effective groups experiencing disappointment.

Aggression in Sports:

Aggression is behavior and activities that normally look to incur psychological and additionally physical damage, either on someone else or on a person's assets or darlings. Physiologists utilize tow terms to mean differentiating thought processes in aggressing. Retaliatory aggression signifies behavior occupied with by people endeavoring to do physical or psychological damage to other people. Instrumental aggression means activities that reflect just making a decent attempt and utilizing extraordinary exertion, with out going with wants to harm someone else.

A few examinations center around aggression whether it is acquired behavior DI not. Lorenz (1966) and Audrey (1966) guarantee, based on broad creature examines, that since aggression, as other creature behaviors, is natural and a prerequisite of animal varieties endurance, and since man advanced from the lower creatures actuation to aggression should be a sense in man as well. In any case, Bin passage Montagu (1968) and Russell have contended that ethologists have almost no strong proof from creature concentrates in normal settings and that aggression in bondage is identified with Crowding and the subsequent breakdown of the social request.

In sports circumstance, numerous researches have been done to discover the significance of aggression and to distinguish who will be the more aggressive at the hour of competition is (member or non-member). Gaebelin and Taylor (1971) recommend that competition increment the status of members to react aggressively. Backing to his is found in investigation of Ryan (1970) who discovered tangle crushed subjects were bound to aggress than champs.

Berkowtiz (1952) says dissatisfaction and ecological factors are the reason for aggression. In this proposition, the probability of the presence of outer can be that inspires the aggression and gives an objective was examined. These presumptions have been tried by Benkowtiz and Geen (1966) subjects were either maddened or treated impartially and afterward shown movies of either a severe bout or a current track race. Also, an endeavor was made to control the prompt estimation of the provocateurs by naming one of them after a character in the fight. The consolidated impacts of outrage, aggressive, modeling from the film and aggressive naming delivered the most elevated level of aggression.

Ogilive and Tutko (1964) have contemplated Olympic swimmers, track athletes, volleyball players, engine hustling drivers and numerous other high level contenders. Regarding the 16 P.F. results fruitful sportsmen were high on factor E (strength), F (surgency), I (contact mindedness) - demonstrating general aggressiveness-and on C (steadiness), O (certainty) a Qz (self - adequacy) In England Kane (1970) has supported a large number of these discoveries and reasons that they consider a working depiction of the sportsman as a steady and aggressive outgoing person.

Volkamer (1971) recommends that aggressive demonstrations are bound to happens when a group is losing, playing away from home, or possesses a low situation in the alliance, when the sore is low, and when a high-positioning group meets a low-positioning group. Pilz (1979) found that exceptionally effective players of both group handball and soccer/football held more inspirational perspectives about submitting aggressive demonstrations than did less fruitful athletes in these sports.

All the investigations show that aggression in sport has been discovered to be useful on occasion, communicated by cautious players whose outflows of expertise need not be exact. In any case, exorbitant aggression beside its ethical ramifications might be not exactly valuable when significant degrees of expertise are required. Aggression in sport is formed by the obtaining of remunerations. Winning and love, cash just as social standards that approves aggression in different sports and sport circumstances.

Also, a person's ethical inclination may form whether the individual overlooks aggression by others in sport and whether the individual communicates exorbitant aggression in sport.

Moore (1966) consider psychoanalytic translation of sport innocuous social outlet toddler just for the players' aggressions yet in addition for the fans is an astounding illustration of how-a particular closed minded hypothetical conceptualization of the world can dazzle one to unmistakably verifiable realities. In spite of Moore's perceptions, out breaks of savagery and Mass revolting at sporting occasions are all around normal wonders all through the world.

An assortment of studies have examined the connection between aggressive behavior and roundabout or vicarious interest. Like review different types of physical movement (Hartman, 1969 Turner, 1970, Goldstein and Arms, 1971, Leith, (1978), different examinations (Husman, 1955 Volkames, 1972, Lefbree and Masses, 1974 Leith, 1978 Ailway, 1978 soliman, 1978) explored the connection between aggressive behavior and direct support in different types of physical action.

Representative, 1974, recognized two sorts of aggression, relative and instrumental receptive or hostile aggression is the conveyance of physical or psychological punishnent as an end instead of a methods (Silva. 1979:202) Bertowitz (1965) calls it "irate aggression" in light of the fact that the attacker is regularly irritated with the objective of the demonstration, "with both view of the other individual as a danger of harmful boosts and the feeling of outrage being fundamental concomitants" (Alderman, 1974: 229). Instrumental aggression includes a goal to perpetrate agony, or injury as an unfortunate obligation substantial compensation as cash, triumph or acclaim Silva, 1979).

Sex Difference in Sports:

There are clear social and sex contrasts in the support accommodated aggressive behavior. This is reflected in sport in an unmistakable contrast between the support accommodated males and females in their aggression. In equal design, western culture additionally will in general rebuff females for aggressive behavior to a lot more prominent. Stanworth found that young ladies as often as possible under-assessed theirs, especially when contrasting themselves with young ladies. Young ladies additionally would in general attribute their victories to karma or exertion, yet their disappointments to absence of capacity. On the off chance that a young lady succeeds she will in general portray herself as fortunate, which conveys no expectations of future achievement, or as a hand laborer who isn't really talented. In the event that she fizzles on the other and this is a result of absence of capacity, not on the grounds that she didn't buckle down enough or was unfortunate.

Work on female athletes doesn't show a comparative example. Blucker and Hischberges audit a few investigations, which have shown no sex contrasts in causal attribution's in sports circumstances. They infer that sports ladies ought not be relied upon to adjust to standards found in the overall female populace since they are a profoundly self - chose gathering. They are more hermaphroditic, and bisexuality and has been demonstrated to be identified with apparent inner control in females. Male/female people have been discovered to be higher in self-regard than non-hermaphroditic people. They likewise mention that person who follows the normal example of female outside progress, attributions would presumably not be found in cutting edge athletic projects.

The male competitor is described by extraversion and passionate dependability and scores high on fait proportions of strength, social aggression, initiative, touch mindedness, security and certainty (Kana, 1972). He works at low degree of uneasiness (Ogilivie, et al. 1971) Gupta and Sharma (1976) discovered athletes to be sincerely expressive, co-employable, versatile, liberal, striking and disorderly.

Investigations of Morgan, (1979), Morgan and Pollock (1977) demonstrated effective athletes to be less restless, less tense, less befuddle, less discouraged furious or not so much exhausted but rather more psychologically overwhelming in examination with less fruitful athletes.

Fletcher (1971) utilized the E. P. P. S. furthermore, discovered undeniable degrees of secondary school athletic interest to be emphatically identified with high association, heterosexuality, aggression, presentation and predominance however contrarily identified with concession, request, succedanea, dishonor and perseverance.

Peterson et al. (1967) Administered the 16 PF test to first class female athletes and discovered them tc be more steady genuinely more canny more faithful, really safeguarding and more aggressive. Unexpectedly, singular athletes were discovered to be more withdrawn than team activity athletes. Mahmood (1981) discovered athletes to be more self-guaranteed, certain and loose than non-athletes.

Devi Balsakrishnan and Dhandpani (1978) endeavors to discover the character contrasts that may exist between athletes of track field and group activities on the three measurement viz., self preoccupation, extraversion, neuroticism and psychoticism, proposed by Eysenck (1976). The example comprised of 90 athletes, 30 for track sports, 30 for field sports and 30 for group activities. A single direction examination of fluctuation and 't' test processed uncovered group activities athletes to contrast essentially from olympic style events sports athletes on all the three measurements.

Gill et al, 1984) inspected the hopes, performance, gotten capacity and causal attributions of males and females who contended on an engine task in the wake of being coordinated with an equivalent - or other gender rival of comparable capacity. Males were almost certain than females to foresee a success in competition, yet genuine performance estimates post-competition capacity evaluations and attributions uncovered more sure reactions to competition by females than males.

Females improved their performance times and raised their capacity appraisals from the underlying nor-serious meeting more than males and spot, more significance on impact attributions than males. The discoveries propose that competition isn't really adverse and behaviors when the serious undertaking and circumstance are unmistakably suitable from females.

Dyer (1976) examines the social effects on female competitor and swimming performance. He distinguished the social factors as differential arrangement of offices and consolation of sport by schooling specialists, representatives and people in general everywhere in various nations. Dyer (1976) analyzed people performances in these nations. As hereditary an ecological factors in any one nation would have equivalent significance to males and females in that country contrast between the general degrees of accomplishment of people in various nations would seen to be sign of the activity of more inconspicuous social factors. For example, ladies in various nations sight be empowered differentially, and have diverse assumption for their latent capacity and capacities. These factors would impact their interest and thus their accomplishment levels.

Individuals from social framework for the most part debilitate developments against others except if it is coordinated against wellsprings of danger. Such behavior is regularly portrayed as aggression. Buss (1961), an outstanding scientist in the field of aggression, keeps up that aggression is a reaction that conveys negative improvements to another creature having its underlying foundations in the disappointment. The dissatisfaction that outcomes because of a square in seeking after an objective not just creates aggressive inclinations among individuals particularly among the youths, yet additionally uplifts the aggressive emotionality relying on the force of apparent disappointment. Consequently the negative conditions like disappointment, antagonism and disdain collector more prominent consideration in examining and breaking down the life systems of aggression.

It is accepted that aggression is cultivated not just by a solitary factor, rather it is discovered to be a result of the cooperation of a few conditions in the social request. Hardship, being a social condition works conspicuously in making men more aggressive. Further it is accepted that aggression represents an incredible danger to the development and advancement of human possibilities. Subsequently the individuals who are presented to the various degrees of hardship are found to communicate assortment of aggressive demonstrations. The majority of the exploration on aggression is centered around hardship of parental relationship and child raising examples. It is seen that, the nature of parent-child relationship is found to impact the improvement of the child's character. Singes, Maccoby and Levin (1957) have seen that guardians who utilized physical discipline had the children who were more aggressive and rough. Obviously aggressive behavior of the guardians filled in as a model for their child s behavior (Bandura and Walter, 1963).

Agarwal and Pandey (1985) announced the impacts of friendship hardship on the ancestral children. This report uncovers the significance of love needed by a child to have an ostensible existence. The higher the friendship hardship, more prominent the disappointment among the children. One of the significant occasions in the existence of an individual is the connection that the structures with mother and other huge others. In 1951, a paper for the World Health Organization by John Bowlby proposed that, maternal hardship could be a significant reason for some social, enthusiastic and scholarly issues. A comparable investigation of Paul Mussen (1961) uncovers that gross disregard, misuse and outrageous hardship of warmth in early stages and childhood may bring about transitory or in any event, suffering aggression. The turn of events and change of the needs of the individual mirror his encounters of need satisfaction and disappointment. All dissatisfaction makes aggression. Dissatisfaction is the aftereffect of some power meddling with the advancement towards an objective.

Eduarda, Concepcion and Aurelia (1992) have announced that family savagery is a great determinant of adolescent maladjusted that outcomes in intense aggression. Bjorkqvist Kaj and Osterman (1992) examined the parental impact on children's self assessed aggressiveness, and detailed that the passionate relationship, for young men, was a higher priority than the genuine behavior of the guardians. Fathers were a higher priority than the moms in creating aggressiveness in young ladies. Subsequently parental impact is additionally a factor in the improvement of aggressive propensities among the youths.

Joe and John 11992) contemplated the impact of family relationship regarding parental separation on aggression of youth. The Buss-Durkee Hostility-Guilt stock was utilized to consider the aggression of youth. The outcomes showed that young men scored higher on attack while the young ladies scored higher on circuitous antagonism. Accordingly children of jump reed guardians scored higher on aggression. This shows the significance of parental relations in forming the behavior of the children.

Robert Alison and Jane (1993) analyzed whether aggressive behavior in preschool was all the more firmly identified with singular attributes of the child, as surveyed at home, to parts of mother-child collaboration. Clearly, subjects whose moms utilized warmth and control all the more sufficiently showed minimal aggression in preschool. Hardship of loving mother child relationship lead to the critical result, for example, disappointment of the children to show typical relationship with others and need moral duty.

Many exploration discoveries show that aggressiveness will in general be a normally male trademark. Males of some random species are more aggressive than females (Scott, 1958). Sharma and Nagaich (1983) contemplated the connection between sex dissatisfaction modalities of understudies and found that ladies were more influenced by disappointment through relapse, obsession and abdication, while men responded through aggression. Besides, males are less liable and on edge about participating in aggressive behaviors.

Dominic A. et.al, (1984) examined the verbal aggression as a component of the collectors pugnacity and inferred that males favored more verbal aggression contrasted with females. A comparable report by Colbert (1993) reports that males scored altogether higher than females on verbal aggression. Yet, numerous investigations have presumed that male favor more physical aggression contrasted with female who lean toward verbal aggression (Mirja, 1992).

Eagly and Steffen (1984) reason that males seem, by all accounts, to be more aggressive than females relying on relevant foundation. The thing that matters was more articulated in examinations including non-physical type of aggression i.e., verbal attacks. The thing that matters is huge in circumstances where aggression appeared to be required as opposed to unreservedly picked (Eagly and Steffen, 1986).

Cairns Robert (1986) examined aggression among young ladies and young men and bite the dust results uncovered that young men are more aggressive than young ladies and aggression expanded with age. Individuals are aware of social endorsement for their behaviors which may reduce the measure of aggression. Anyway with increment old enough individuals may not be made a fuss over the social endorsement, which appears to give more aggressive behavior.

In an endeavor of investigating sex contrasts in aggressive propensities, Robensteim Feldman, S. Shirley, Robin and Noveekira (1987) made a culturally diverse investigation of drawings of children and found that young men drew more topics of aggression, competition and strength than did the young ladies. Mc Cabe Allyssa and Lipscomb Thomos (1988) examined sex distinction in children's verbal aggression. The outcomes uncovered no sex contrast in verbal aggression in early period however later there was generous increment with age in the extent of verbal aggression: Boys were more aggressive than young ladies and utilized more aggressive remarks.

Gladue mind '1991) contemplated the aggressive behavioral attributes in people, and uncovered that male announced more physical and verbal aggression and had lighter scores on proportions of hastiness and pool of disappointment resistance than females.

Harris (1992) made an expounded investigation of sex, race and experience of aggression. It is seen that males have displayed a greater number of types of aggressive behavior than the females. Blacks have shown more physical aggression while whites have communicated non-physical aggression.

Arnold Buss (1963) in the wake of considering physical aggression according to various dissatisfactions reached be resolution that the sex distinction in force of aggression was predictable with the broadly held conviction that the men were more aggressive than the ladies. Anyway he saw a novel sex distinction regarding subject-casualty collaboration; that is the men aggressed more against men man against ladies, however the ladies aggressed similarly against people.

John and David (1985) contemplated the impact of sexual orientation name on the impression of aggress on in children. At the point when the assailant was named as male the children saw him as more aggressive than when he was named as female. This completely uncovers that men are seen to be an emblematic for aggressive demonstrations.

Campbell et al, (1997) analyzed the degree of backhanded aggression among people and found that ladies scored higher than men on circuitous aggression. It is concurred that circuitous expressive aggression neglects to show relationship with social portrayal since it does not have the proper necessity of purposeful damage and thus isn't a demonstration of aggression.

Ujjwala Rani and Ramavani (1989) contemplated age distinction in articulation of aggression in people. Results showed that age and sex have huge free impact on articulation of aggression. The two people express their aggression, however ladies express aggression without harming their delicate female picture, where as men express aggression in more straightforward and dynamic manners. Anyway ladies are less aggressive than men just under specific conditions, particularly when ladies accept that such behavior is wrong and conflicting with female sex job. In circumstances where such controls are missing, distinction between the genders may diminish or even may evaporate completely.

Rozario, Kapur, Rao and Dalai (1994) contemplated the example of psychological aggravations of young people young men and young ladies and presumed that aggressive behavior was more common among young men when contrasted with young ladies. Appropriately young men experience more psychological unsettling influences than young ladies because of aggressive demonstrations that are available in more degrees.

An analysis directed by Richardson, Bernstein and Tailor (1979) proposes that others will see the moderately low degree of aggression frequently appeared by female's come from their conviction that such behavior as sex unseemly. Along these lines the sex contrast in aggression which are for the most part because of sex job guidelines are progressively evolving.

Basu (1991) investigated the aggressive reactions of male and female children and found that the sex of the disappointed figure influenced the sort and bearing of aggression in both male and female subjects.

Kundu and Chaudhuri (1989) analyzed the aggressive response designs in 100 young men and 100 young ladies and found that sex of the subjects influenced the response examples of aggression Boys were discovered to be more aggressive than the girls.

Colbert Kent (1993) saw that verbal aggression was essentially higher in males than females. Nolen (1994) found that young ladies show fundamentally higher paces of burdensome issues than the young men. The sex contrasts were because of certain wild stress in early pre-adulthood. Young ladies face more negative life occasions and social conditions, consequently, they display more detached adapting styles of aggression.

Another variable that appears to impact the aggressive behavior is the sex. It is accepted that sex related behavior is discovered to be related with the aggression that is shown. All the more conspicuously males of some random society are accepted to communicate more aggressive demonstrations than the females. Anyway females similarly have an edge over males in the statement of.

CHAPTER-IV

METHODOLOGY

OBJECTIVES

The following are the objectives of the present study:

1.   To study the influence of aggression on sports performance.

2.   To study the influence of self concept on sports performance of persons.

3.   To study the sex difference in sports performance.

4.   To study the variation of psychological factors in two age groups and their influence on sports performance.

Statement of the Problem:

To assess the study on aggression, self concept and motor ability on the sports persons

HYPOTHESES

The following hypotheses are set for the study:

1.   There is an influence of aggression on sports performance.

2.   There would be significant differences in psycho factors between the two sample sub-groups of age and sex.

3.   There is a significant influence of self concept on sports performance.

4.   There are sex differences in the sports performance of   sample sub-groups.

5.   There will be significant difference in sports performance between two age groups.

Significance of study

The study makes an endeavor to survey the influence of various psychological factors on sports performance. It is surely known that psychological factors are profoundly between identified with sports activities. Knowing the significant influence of factors, a game psychologist or sports educationist can control these psychological factors to improve the performance of sports persons. This application is significant commitment to the field of sports according to sports performance.

The setting:

Keeping significant objectives of the study in see, proper plan was is received. The study was led on 300 sports persons chose from different colleges of Gulbarga. The basis of choice was investment in sports at any rate at intercollegiate level. In this manner the sample chose was arranged similarly on variables like age and sex. The conveyance of sample is given in Table-1.

Table-1

Distribution of Sample

Age	Male	Female	Total
15-20 Years (Gr.l)	75	75	150
21 & above Years (Gr.2)	75	75	150
Total	**150**	**150**	**300**

The sample so chose was administrated the scales, viz, aggression and self concept. This is done to inspect the contrasts between the sample' sub-bunches on psycho factor and thusly the sample was sorted dependent on the scores on psycho factors to get to impact of free factor on the sports performance of the respondents. Since the sports performance is fairly affected by the psycho factors of the members.

Since the study endeavors to evaluate the impact of psychological factors on sports performance of the sample, the psychological factors like aggression and self concepts (SC), were treated as free variables that are accepted to influence motor performance of sports persons. The performance of sample subgroups classified as reliant variable was estimated in three distinctive motor occasions of 100 meters, 200 meters and 400 meters.

TOOLS:

The following tests are used in the present study:

1. **Aggression Inventory:** This inventory was initially evolved by Bus-Durkee (1957) and was restandardized by Ujwalarani and Rama Rao (1988). There are 60 things with valid or bogus other options. The things are scored with the assistance of scoring key given in the manual. As needs be, higher scores demonstrate higher level of aggression and vice-versa. The dependability of the scale is 0.92 (part half).

2. **Self Concept Scale:** This scale is created by Saraswat, R.K. (1984) which comprises of 48 things with five other options. The scoring is of Likert type (summated rating). The higher score uncovers higher self concept and vice-versa. The dependability of the scale is 0.815 (part half) which is significant.

Statistical Techniques:

The statistical methods and tools that are employed in this study are as follows:

1. t-test is used to analyze contrasts between sample subgroups.

2. Correlation test - r is used to study the correlation among the variables.

3. ANOVA is used to evaluate the influence of independent variables on the dependant variable.

CHAPTER-V

DISCUSSION OF RESULTS

5.1. Comparison of Sample Subgroups on psychological Factors

As stated in the earlier chapter the sample of the study is drawn from Gulbarga and the chose respondents were balanced as far as sex and age (Table-1 appropriation of sample). The significant objective of the study has been to survey the effect of psychological factors like aggression and self concept on the performance in 100 meters, 200 meters, and 400 meters motor occasion. Anyway it is felt essential of analyze the sub-gatherings of age and sex on the psycho factors to inspect the degree to which the psycho factors separate the sample sub-gatherings of age and sex. It was thought proper to know the distinctions in the sports performance of the respondents by classifying based on psycho factors along these lines.

In this way, in the first place, an endeavor is made to look at the degree to which the respondents contrast on psycho factors. This can be accomplished by registering the mean scores of psycho factors on two sample sub-gatherings of age and sex. The information are orchestrated and introduced in the accompanying tables.

Table-2

Mean, SD and t-value of self concept in male-female sub-group (N=300)

Sex		High SC	Low SC	t-value
Male	M	206.08	71.40	** 80.16
	SD	25.01	11.9	
	N	85	65	
Female	M	198.11	80.59	** 36.9
	SD	21.2	15.31	
	N	61	89	
t-value		2.06*	4.17**	

* Significant at 0.05 level.
** Significant at 0.01 level.

The mean, SD and t-values of self concept in male-female class is introduced in Table-2. It tends to be seen that the male respondents have scored a mean of 206.08 in high self concept while the females have scored a mean 198.11. The t-esteem is 2.06 which is significant at 0.05 level. In low self concept, the male respondents have scored lower means (71.40) than females (80.59).

It tends to be seen through Table-2, that both male (N=150) and female (N=150) respondents are named having a place with the classification of high self concept and low self concept. This is done dependent on the standards of the SC scale Mean, SD and t-values of self concept in male-female sub-gathering (N=300) (Sarswath 1984) which unmistakably clarifies that one who scores over 193 is delegated having a place with high self concept while the person who scores under 48 is named having a place with low self concept classification all in all. As needs be, there are 85 males and 61 females with high self concept and 65 males and 89 females with low self concept in low self concept class. Again the t-esteem (4.17) is significant at 0.01 level. Hence obviously there are significant sex contrasts in both the classifications of self concept. In this manner male respondents nave more coordinated perceptions, convictions, and mentalities than those of female partners. In this manner self concept which is an individual trait of oneself is found to create more significant sex contrasts in the example of the investigation. This is valid if there should be an occurrence of low self concept class additionally where in the individualistic perception is discovered to be low in female sub-gatherings. Further there are likewise significant contrasts among high and low self concept in male just as female sub-bunches as the t-values are significant past 0.01 level. This obviously talks that there are unmistakable contrasts in the individualistic concepts among the example of male and female. Chart 1 strikingly clarifies the equivalent.

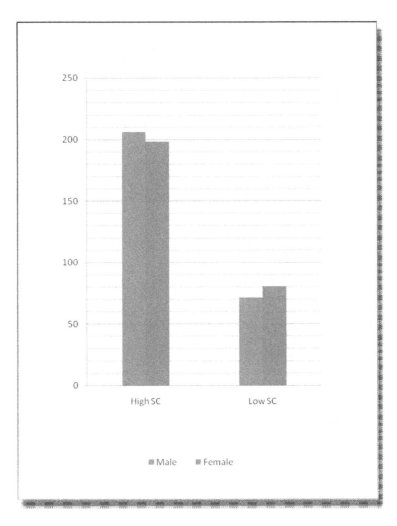

Graph-1
Self Concept in Male-Female Sub-groups

Table-3

Mean, SD and t-value of Aggression in male-female

sub-group (N=300)

Sex		High aggression	Low aggression	t-value
Male	M	105.78	34.03	** 21.66
	SD	29.15	9.99	
	N	93	57	
Female	M	93.21	28.12	** 21.98
	SD	22.22	7.21	
	N	61	89	
t-value		3.06**	3.83**	

** Significant at 0.01 level.

In Table-3 the information of male - female sub-bunch is given. As indicated by the standards one who scores higher than middle score of 41 (Buss Darky) is supposed to be high forceful and the other way around. As needs be, there are 93 males in high aggression, 57 in Low aggression and there are 61 females in high aggression and 89 in low aggression.

It is noticed tangle the mean score of male in high aggression is 105.78 and that of females is 93.21. The t-esteem (3.06) is significant at 0.01 level. This unmistakably demonstrates that there are significant sex contrasts in high aggression category. Apparently the size of aggression is an element of sex sound system composed job moreover. Also there are significant higher scores of males in low aggression than the female as the t-esteem in this category is significant. There are additionally significant contrasts between the high and low forceful inclinations with the sample gatherings. Subsequently it is discovered that aggression is a potential factor that produces significant contrasts among male and female sample. As such, there are significant sex contrasts in the aggression. Similar outcomes are introduced in Graph-2.

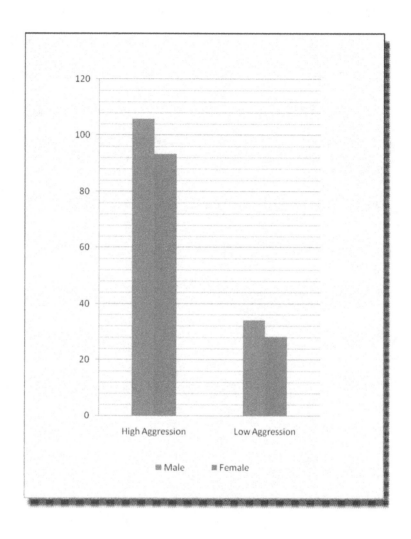

Graph-2
Aggression in Male-Female Sub-group

<u>**Table-4**</u>

Mean, SD and t-value of Self Concept in Junior-Senior Sub-group (N-300)

Category		High SC	Low SC	t-value
Juniors Age Gr-1 (15-20)	M	180.2	70.2	** 16.44
	SD	19.1	12.5	
	N	90	60	
Seniors Age Gr-2 (21 and above)	M	196.9	69.2	** 45.8
	SD	20.5	13.1	
	N	85	65	
t-value		**5.54****	**0.43**	

** Significant at 0.01 level.

The mean, SD and t-values of self concept in two distinctive age groups are introduced in Table-4. As can be seen the mean scores of youngsters in high self concept category is 180.02 and that of seniors is 196.9. The t-estimation of 5.54 is significant at 0.01 level. Unmistakably the high self concept produces significant contrasts between the two age groups. Clearly the senior respondents (21 or more age) have strikingly unique in association of perceptions, perspectives and values. Anyway the lesser sub-gathering however having a place with high self concept category have moderately lower perceptual designs that portrayed, self concept.

Anyway in low self concept category there are no significant contrasts between the two sample sub-gathering old enough. Yet, there are significant contrasts among high and low self concept groups with the sample inside the sub-gathering of youngsters and seniors as the t-values which are significant uncover. Along these lines self concept is discovered to be a significant factor in having an effect between the respondents of two age groups. Graph-3 plainly clarifies this reality.

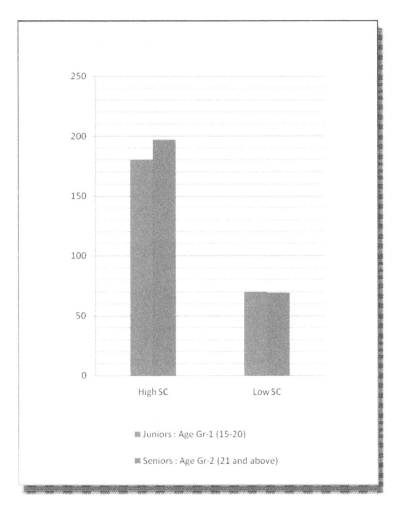

Graph-3
Self Concept in Two Groups of Age

Table - 5
Mean, SD and t-values of Aggression in Junior-Senior Sub-group (N-300)

Category		High Aggression	Low Aggression	t-value
Juniors Age Gr-1	M	98.11	33.80	22.9**
	SD	23.10	8.5	
	N	80	70	
Seniors Age Gr-2	M	85.01	30.00	**36.24
	SD	19.22	7.9	
	N	82	68	
t-value		3.89**	2.70*	

** Significant at 0.01 level.

Table-5 presents mean, SD and t-value of aggression in two sample sub-groups of age. It very well may be seen that the mean scores of juniors is (98.11) significantly higher in high aggression class than those of senior (85.01) partners. The t-value of 3.89-is significant at 0.01 level which demonstrates that there are significant contrasts among junior and senior respondents in high aggression. Additionally the juniors have outscored seniors in low aggression as the significant t-value uncovers. There likewise contrasts among high and low aggression with junior and senior sample sub-bunch as the t-values are past 0.01 level. Hence the outcomes completely highlight that aggression produces noticeable contrasts in the members having a place with two age groups.

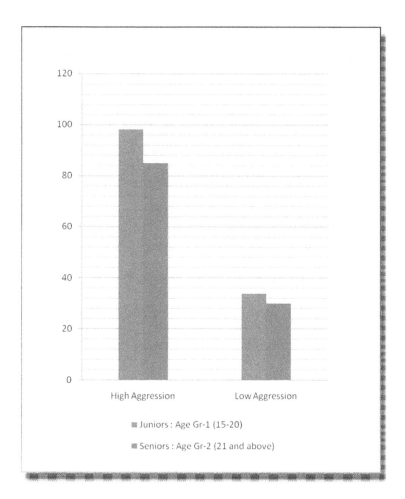

Graph-4
Aggression in two Groups of Age

Psychological Factors and Sports Performance

The major objective of the study has been to evaluate the effect of psycho factors on the performance of sports persons or people. It is accepted that the presentation of competitors is basically controlled by the mental factors such as self concept and aggression. Moreover, the age of the player, plays ar. significant job in the accomplishment of higher motor performance. The performance is surveyed regarding time (in a moment or two) taken by major part in occasions like 100 meters, 200 meters and 400 meters speed. Appropriately the person who takes lesser time is accepted to have the better presentation generally. In this way it is fundamental for depict the effect of psycho factors on the exhibition of competitors. For the reason the sample has been classified dependent on free factors. The information was exposed to factual examination and the overall remaining of the sample sub-groups was resolved with the assistance of mean scores. In this manner the outcomes so arranged are introduced in the Tables.

Table-6

Mean SD and t-values of Motor ability Performance in

Two Categories of Age (N = 300)

Category		100 mtrs.	200 mtrs.	400 mtrs.
Juniors Age-Group-1	M	13.60	30.69	59.12
	SD	998	2.19	3.76
	N	151	151	151
Seniors Age-Gioup-2	M	15.91	33.22	63.72
	SD	9.96	2-75	4.61
	N	149	149	149
t-value		2.83**	8.78**	9.45**

**Significant at 0.01 level

Table-6 exhibits the means, SD, and t values of sports performance in three occasions of 100 meters, 200 meters, and 400 meters speed of sports persons in two age groups (Juniors and Seniors). It very well may be seen that in case of 100 meters run the performances of juniors is superior to those of senior competitors. The juniors have scored a mean of 13.60 while the seniors have a mean of 15.91. Plainly the juniors have taken less time in case of 100 meters speed test. The acquired t-value of 2.83 that is significant at 0.01 level which uncovers that there are significant contrasts in the athletic performance between the two sample sub-groups. Clearly the competitors having a place with the age gathering of 15-20 have significantly higher performance than their partners.

It very well may be seen that the juniors gathering (Age Group-1) has taken a mean of 30.69 in 200 meters occasion while the seniors have scored a mean of 33.22 This uncovers that juniors lave taken moderately lesser time in the finishing of given sports task than those of seniors. The acquired t-value of 8.78 which is significant at 0.01 level plainly uncovers that there are significant contrasts in the sports performance between the players having a place with various age groups. The juniors with part of spirit and enthusiasm have outperformed their more established partners in the speed test. Consequently apparently age is an unmistakable factor in delivering more contrasts in the sports performance between the competitors having a place with various age groups: bring down the age more prominent is sports performance. Prior examinations have seen the comparative outcomes were in juniors consistently are in front of their seniors in the given sports rivalry.

Along these lines the lesser sample bunch has outperformed the seniors in 400 meters speed test. In this occasion likewise the senior sample bunch has significantly lower performance than the lesser partners, as the got the mean scores uncover. The t-value on this occasion is significant at 0.01 level which, obviously shows the significant contrasts between groups on 400 meters speed test. Chart 9 clarifies this all the more plainly.

The facts demonstrate that the speed test requires parcel of enthusiasm, spirit, and energy. The age is additionally a factor in imparting the possible essential for the accomplishment of higher sports performance. It's implied that the lower age bunch consistently over toss the higher age bunch in the athletic occasions. Thus the juniors are found to have a ton of life and endurance in outscoring the more established ones. This is especially obvious if there should be an occurrence of occasions including speed performance. Subsequently, it very well may be contended that the game individual having a place with the age gathering of 15 - 20 performs better compared to those having a place higher age gathering. Subsequently the members of junior age bunch have shown significantly higher athletic performance than their partners.

As has been expressed before, the sports performance is to a great extent controlled by the psychological factors of the players. In the current examination the factors like, self concept and aggression are treated as psychological factors which are accepted to apply more noteworthy impact on the performance of sports persons. In like manner the information identified with psychological factors are set up on classified sample dependent on free variables and introduced in the Tables.

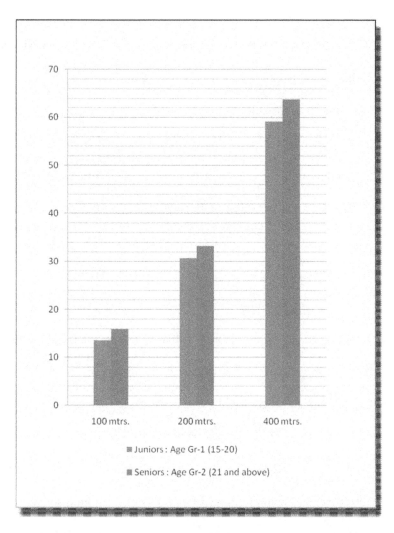

Graph-5
Sports Performance of Motor ability in Two categories of Age

Table-7

Mean, SD and t-values of Motor ability Performance in Two Categories of Self Concept (N=300)

Self Concept		100 mtrs.	200 mtrs.	400 mtrs.
Low	M	15.90	33.19	63.68
	SD	10.00	2.72	4.56
	N	148	148	148
High	M	13.63	30.74	39.18
	SD	1.01	2.27	3.89
	N	152	152	152
t-value		2.79**	8.45**	9.20**

** Significant at 0.01 level.

Table-7 shows the Mean, SD and t-values of engine capacity performance of 100, 200 and 400 meters engine in two classes of self concept. It tends to be seen that the sports persons of high self concept have significantly lower means (13.63) than those of low self concept (15.90) in 100 mtrs. engine. The lower mean demonstrates the better performance and the other way around. It is seen that the members having positive self concept have performance better than the self concept members. The acquired t-value of 2.79 which is significant as 0.01 level uncovers the way that there are significant contrasts in the performance between the two samples of groups in 100 Mtrs. speed test. In this manner self concept as a psychological factor is discovered to be a likely factor in delivering the significant contrasts in the sports performance between the individuals who have higher self concept and who have lower.

It is seen that the respondents with high self concept have scored a mean of 30.74 and those with low self concept have a mean of 33.19 in 200 meters occasion. In this manner the time taken by the sample of high self concept is lower than that of low self concept. The t-value of 8.45 which is significant at 0.01 level uncovers that there are significant contrasts in sports performance 200 meters run between the respondents of high and low self concept. The higher self concept that enthuses and ingrains the positive image of oneself is conspicuous factor in driving an individual for the accomplishment of any engine segment Consequently a person with positive self concept is accepted to dominate the one with low self concept in any speed test. Consequently the outcomes high light the way that self concept is a significant psychological consider that causes contrasts the performance of competitors. Essentially the previous investigations have supported the equivalent.

A comparable pattern can be seen in 400 meters where by the games with higher self concept are found to accomplish preferred performance over those with lower self concept. The t-values in this occasion is significant past 0.01 level to demonstrate the noticeable contrasts between two sample sub-groups. Accordingly the outcomes classifications articulate that the sports performance is to a great extent intervened by the psychological factor such as self concept, which drives sports persons for better accomplishment. The self concept that instigates self certainty and self mage, accepted to administer the over all performance of the people. Consequently higher the self concept more prominent is the sports performance. Clearly the outcomes suggest the way that higher self concept is a sponsor portion to the performance of players. Essentially, Graph-6 uncovers the equivalent.

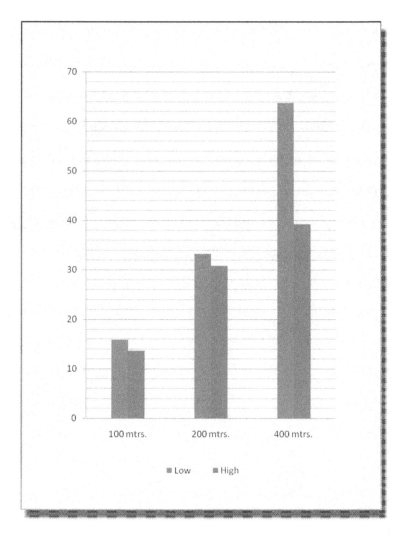

Graph-6
Motor ability Performance in two categories of Self concept

Table-8

Mean SD and t-values of Motor ability Performance in

Aggression (N = 300)

Aggression		100 mtrs.	200 mtrs.	400 mtrs.
Low	M	15.89	33.20	63.46
	SD	10.21	2.83	4.80
	N	142	142	142
High	M	13.73	30.82	59.56
	SD	1.09	2.20	3.97
	N	158	158	158
t-value		2.64*	8.14**	7.68**

*Significant at 0.05 level
** Significant at 0.01 level

The mean, SD and t-values of sports persons in various engine occasions is introduced in Table-8. It tends to be seen that the players with higher aggression have a mean of 13.73 while players with low aggression have a mean of 15.98 in 100 mtrs. race. This uncovers that higher forceful sample of gathering have significantly lower scores than that of low aggression bunch as the t-value of 2.64 which is significant at 0.05 level shows. In this manner aggression is a factor found to create the significant distinction in the performances of games. In 200 meters occasion the mean score of low forceful gathering is 33.20 while the higher forceful gathering has a mean of 30.82. This uncovers that the sample high aggression has taken significantly lower time in the speed test than that of lower aggression as the t-value of 8.14 which is significant at 0.01 level shows. Accordingly aggression is discovered to be a psychological factor that propells competitor's performance. The facts confirm that specific measure of aggression is a fundamental fixing in the accomplishment of any speed task. It readies the player with a spirit of greatness and puts forth to place fitting attempts to make progress engine test requires the psycho-physiological association that prepares the competitor for cooperation and achievement. Clearly the improvement in the performance is administered by the psychological factor like aggression. Numerous investigations inspected loan backing to this factor. Essentially the higher aggression bunch has preferable performances over the low aggression bunch in the other occasion of 400 meters as the t-value on this occasion which is significant at 0.01 level shows. Diagram 11 plainly clarifies this.

In this way the higher performance is discovered to be controlled by the aggression that a sports man forces and express. The aggression is in this manner, a fundamental factor in any sports rivalry. As a psychological factor the aggression of sports man helps in the accomplishment of higher athletic scores. Along these lines it very well may be said that the aggression in sports has an instrumental value is improve the sports performance.

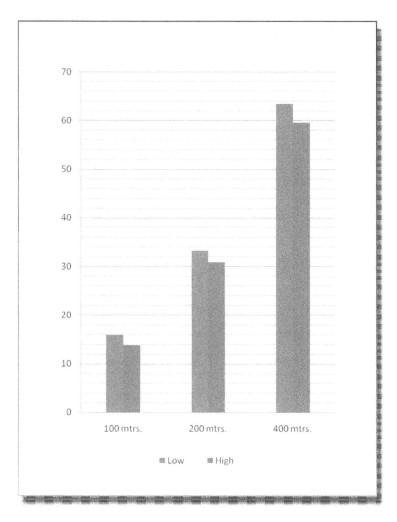

Graph-7
Motor ability Performance in Two Categories of Aggression

Table-9

Mean, SD and t-value of Motor ability Performance in Male-Female Sub-group (N=300)

Category		100 mtrs.	200 mtrs.	400 mtrs.
Male	M	13.93	30.95	59.84
	SD	1.15	2.69	4.45
	N	150	150	150
Female	M	15.57	32.95	62.97
	SD	9.97	2.15	4.61
	N	150	150	150
t-value		2.606**	6.660*	5.985*

*Significant at 0.05 level
** Significant at 0.01 level

The means SD's and t-values of sports performance is introduced in the Table-9. As can be seen, the mean score of male motor capacity in 100 meters event (13.93) is lower than the mean score of females (15.75). This shows that the guys have taken significantly lower time than their partners in this occasion as the t-value of 2.606 which is significant at 0.05 level infers. Subsequently the performance of male competitors is discovered to be higher than that of females.

In 200 meters events, it is seen that the mean score of male motor capacity is 30.95 and that of females is 32.95. The t-value (6.66) is significant at 0.0) level. This plainly uncovers that guys have taken significantly lesser time than females in the performance. In this manner guys are found to dominate the females in the motor capacity performance. It is generally acknowledged that guys takes consistently lesser time than females in the given motor event. Event the world record set up in the motor events talks about the way that the accomplishment of people in such speed test is extraordinary. Accordingly the outcome completely talk that there are significant sex contrasts in the sports performances between the male and female motor capacity. Something very similar is valid if there should arise an occurrence of 400 meters motor capacity moreover. The previous examinations additionally affirm this. Consequently the consequences of speed articulate that sex belongness is additionally calculated that causes contrast the performance of given sports occasion. The something is graphically introduced in Graph-8 too.

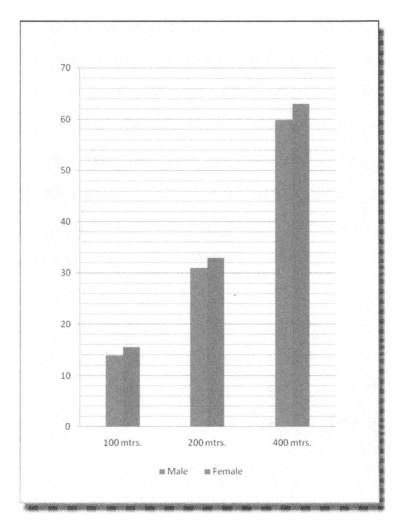

Graph-8
Motor ability Performance in Male-Female Sub-groups

Influence of Independent Variables on Sports Performance

After examining at the distinctions inside the classifications of psycho factors, a further endeavor is made in this segment to evaluate the impact or every free factor on subordinate variable. The psycho factors like, self concept and aggression the factors like age and sex are treated as autonomous variables and the engine performance in 100 meters 200 meters and 400 meters as needy variable. To asses the free impact of every autonomous variable an examination of difference (ANOVA) is figured for 100 meters, 200 meters and 400 meters independently. The F-proportion's for each speed test are given in the accompanying tables.

Table-10

Influence of independent variables on Motor ability performance in
100 meters event : F-ratio (ANOVA) (N=300)

Main effects	SS	DF	MS	F
Aggression	3.138	1	3.138	5.81**
Self concept	1.667	1	1.667	3.98*
Age	23.659	1	23.659	3.84*
Sex	10.3.439	1	103.439	3.85*
INTERACTION				
Agg x SC	3.167	1	3.167	5.02*
Agg x Age	20.312	1	20.312	23.01**
Agg x Sex	99.203	1	99.203	4.9*
SC x Age	19.980	1	19.980	17.97**
SC x Sex	97.214	1	97.214	24.01**
Age x Sex	10K210	1	101.210	36.7**

Table - 16 presents the impact of free variables like aggression.
Self concept age, and sex on engine performance in 100 meters occasion.
It is seen that the F-ratio (5.81) for aggression is significant at 0.01 level,
which shows that aggression affects the performance of respondents in
100 meters speed test. The facts demonstrate that aggress on includes the
inclinations of guard in any opposition. Despite the fact that conceptually
aggression means the inclination to hurt the adversaries, it likewise makes
the player to take conclusive parts to battle any serious circumstance. It is
this traditionalist disposition that supports a major part in field and drives
towards the objective of achievement. Clearly an individual with high
forceful response and motivations is relied upon to acquire benefits in

some random sports performance Therefore it very well may be guessed that aggression is a central player in the accomplishment of field and engine occasions.

The F-ratio for self concept is 3.98 which is significant at 0.05 level to propose the free effect on sports performance of the sample sub-gathering. Plainly self concept as a psychological factor has all the earmarks of being a solid indicator of sports performance. The self concept that comprise of individual perspective on connotes. The example of his reasoning, feeling and carrying on. It is simply the concept that creates self image, self agreement and the personality in the people which at last produce self image, sensation of regard and imparts the self trust in the members. Naturally, an individual higher self concept consistently accomplishes more in correlation with the individuals who have lower self concept. Subsequently it very well may be said that the higher self concept consistently cultivates the performance of the given individual regardless.

The F-ratio for age is 3.84 which is significant at 0.05 level that demonstrates that age is a free affecting element on the engine performance. It is well established actuality that the more youthful age gathering of 15-20 years consistently dominate the members of more seasoned respondent (21 or more age). Accordingly the energy, enthusiasm and spirit that youthful players saturated makes them to accomplish better that their partners.

The F-ratio (3.85) for sex is significant at 0.05 level to demonstrate the autonomous impact on the performance of competitors. Apparently the engine performance in 100 meters of the respondents is administered by the sex-belongingness. The facts confirm that guys consistently out-score females in the "given competitor act. Anyway there are discrete standards the two people independently to decide, the records accomplished by the players. Hence it very well may be said that the higher sports performance is intervened by the sex belongingness of the players.

The association impacts of all the autonomous variable in 100 meter; occasion obviously show that the F-ratio for all the mixes of the free variables are significant. This demonstrates that the performance of competitors is additionally enormously affected by the joined impact of the multitude of sets of autonomous factors. Consequently aggression combined with SC, Age and Sex additionally impacts significantly the engine performance of the sample sub-groups. The factors like SC, aggression, age and sex are to a great extent impacting the engine performance together.

Subsequently, it very well may be presumed that the sports performance in 100 meters is significantly and freely impacted by the autonomous factors like aggression, self concept, age and sex. The previous examinations additionally support the equivalent.

Table-11

Influence of Independent Variables on Motor ability Performance

in 200 meters event F-ratio (ANOVA) (N=300)

Main effects	SS	DF	MS	F
Aggression	10.802	1	10.802	3.912*
Self concept	10.377	1	10.377	3.867*
Age	20.373	1	20,373	6.066**
Sex	167.494	1	167.494	29.615**
INTERACTION				
Agg x SC	12.111	1	12.111	4.20*
Agg x Age	20.410	1	20.410	5.01*
Agg x Sex	32.628	1	32.628	6.01*
SC x Age	21.601	1	21.601	5.82*
SC x Sex	110.001	1	110.001	17,8**
Age x Sex	130.120	1	130.120	23.92**

* Significant at 0.05 level.
** Significant at 0.01 level.

The F-ratio for self concept is 3.867 which is critical at 0.05 level. This uncovers that self concept altogether affects the presentation of athletes in the field and track occasion. It is very unmitigated that the SC which is a coordinated configuration of insight, convictions, feelings, attitudes and qualities empowers a person to see as unmistakable as conceivable from others. It makes self mindfulness around ones qualities and capacities. It additionally produces self image, certainty and understanding which permit an individual to break down the circumstance cautiously and it is this experience that makes an individual to be more touchy to the natural impacts. Accordingly an individual with higher SC is relied upon to accomplish more in assortment of competitive circumstances. This is likewise obvious if there should arise an occurrence of motor field where by motor higher self concept are relied upon to show better than the individuals who have lower self concept.

Table-11 show the impact of independent variable like, aggression and self concept, age and sex on sports execution in 200 meters occasion. Unmistakably the F-ratio for aggression is 3.912 which is critical at 0.05 level to recommend the way that aggression as a psychological variable; has fundamentally impacted the presentation of competitor; in 200 meters speed test. In this manner aggression of the motor is vital in encouraging their sports accomplishment. The players who curve more forceful are found to safeguard that game all the more emphatically and carry the accomplishment to the groups. The traditionalist demeanor motivates the co-players that expansion the solidarity. Accordingly there is a solid connection among players and aggression and objective accomplishment. Consequently, it very well may be reasoned that aggression is a significant psychological factor that incites energy and excitement among the players in any competitive game. Higher the aggression the more noteworthy the sports execution.

Consequently, the results of the examination articulate the way that self concept is a solid component in quickening the sports execution of the players.

Subsequently the results feature the way that the factors like, aggression, self concept, age and sex have affected the motor execution in 200 meters occasion essentially. The prior examinations have additionally noticed the comparable truth.

<u>**Table-12**</u>

Influence of independent variables on motor ability performance

in 400 meters event: F-ratio (ANOVA) (N=300)

Main effects	SS	DF	MS	F
Aggression	85.976	1	85.976	7.285*
Self concept	11.112	1	11.112	4.068*
Age	9.079	1	9.079	3.855**
Sex	437.130	1	437.130	26.869**
INTERACTION				
Agg x SC	61.213	1	61.213	6.98**
Agg x Age	70.614	1	70.614	17.01**
Agg x Sex	210.002	1	210.002	13.92**
SC x Age	225.410	1	225.410	21.01**
SC x Sex	248.313	1	248.313	22.05**
Age x Sex	243.112	1	243.112	25.01**

* Significant at 0.05 level
** Significant at 0.01 level

Table-12 gives F-ratio for free variables like aggression, self concept, age and sex on the engine capacity performance of 400 meters occasion. It can saw that the F-ratio for aggression (85.979) which is significant at 0.01 level shows autonomous effect on sports performance of players. In this way plainly aggression is a significant factor of engine performance. The facts demonstrate that the protective perspectives of a player make more energy, more enthusiasm, more enthusiasm in oneself as well as in others. This makes a group felling or 'we" feeling among the players and serves to quicker he performance in engine. Consequently a player with high forcefulness is found to score more than those with low aggression.

Self concept is another free factor of the investigation. The F-ratio (11.112) for self concept is significant at 0.05 level. This obviously uncovers that concept independently affects the performance in the 400 meters. The self concept which is a coordinated perceptual framework expands one's level of mindfulness, self arrangement and self image, is found to build the appearance of abilities perspectives and acting. Obviously, an individual with high self concept shows more performance than his partners. This is similarly evident if there should arise an occurrence of field and engine occasions where in a player with higher SC outperforms his .partner. Subsequently SC as a psychological variable accepts an unmistakable spot in the clarification of sports conduct.

Age and sex are additionally treated as free variables in the examination. The F-ratio for age is 9.079 and for sex it is 437.130. These F-ratio's are sufficiently significant to recommend that these two factors have autonomous and significant effect on the sports performance in 400 meters occasion. Subsequently the performance of players is additionally administered by their sex belongingness and age. It is seen that the more youthful age bunch has an edge over the more established age bunch in the performance. Essentially male players have outscored females even in this 400 meters engine occasion.

The F-ratio on cooperation impact are on the whole significant to demonstrate the way that the performance of engine capacity in 400 meter test is significantly affected by the joined impact of the multitude of free variables of the examination. It very well may be noticed that the communication impact of the multitude of variables were likewise significant in the event of 100 meters, and 200 meters engine too. Thus, it very well may be presumed that the engine performance of the respondents is-generally a component of free impact of variables, yet in addition is an element of the cooperation impact of these variables on the engine test of the sample sub-groups. Consequently the psycho factors alongside other individual factors noticeably affect the performance both freely and through cooperation. Accordingly psychological factors accept significant in the clarification of sports conduct.

Henceforth the outcomes completely uncover that the engine performance in 100 meters engine is significantly and autonomously affected by free variables like aggression, self concept, age and sex. Very similar things is seen in before concentrates too.

Relationship between Independent Variable and Dependent Variable

It has been grounded that the engine performance in three levels - 100 meters, 200 meters and 400 meters - is to a great extent controlled by the factors like aggression and self concept. These all were treated as psycho factors overseeing the engine performance. It was discovered that every one of these variables were sufficiently likely to create significant diverse in differential sample sub-groups and furthermore were adequately possible to impact significantly and autonomously. In this manner it is demonstrated certain that sports performance - regardless of whether 100 meters, 200 meters, and 400 meters occasion is to a great extent dictated by the commitments of all these psychological factors.

A further endeavor has been made in the investigation analyze to the connection between the psycho factors and engine performance in 100 meters, 200 meters and 400 meters speed test. As needs be the co-relations were registered between psycho variables and ward variable and the revision coefficients (r) are introduced in Table-12.

Table -13

Showing relationship between independent psycho factors and dependent variable.

Sl. No.	Variables	r-values
1.	**Aggression X**	
	a. performance of 100 mtrs.	0.213**
	b. performance of 200 mtrs.	0.312**
	c. performance of 400 mtrs.	0.810**
2.	**Self concept X**	
	a. performance of 100 mtrs.	0.729**
	b. performance of 200 mtrs.	0.816**
	c. performance of 400 mtrs.	0.902**

**Significant at 0.01 level

Table-13 shows the r-values between autonomous factors subordinate variable. It very well may be seen that the r-values among aggression and motor execution in 100 meters, 200 meters and 400 meters are significant at 0.01 levels. This plainly uncovers that aggression is a solid relate of sports execution of motor. The high aggressive respondents have significantly uncovered sports abilities altogether in three events. Subsequently the aggression that makes traditionalist perspectives vital for greatness is discovered to be solid co-related with the exhibition.

The correlation between self concept and sports execution is certainly high as the r-values for all the three events are significant at 0.01 level. Along these lines the higher SC is constantly found to a sponsor portion for athletes in any speed test. Additionally the r-values between friendly help and the sports execution rage significant at 0.01 level to show a positive connection between the two.

Thus, the outcomes completely articulate the way that the psycho factor like, aggression and self concept are the solid corresponds of the motor presentation of players altogether the their motor events of 100 meters, 200 meters, and 400 meters event. The previous investigations have additionally noticed the comparable discoveries.

CHAPTER-VI

SUMMARY AND CONCLUSIONS

Sports are response just as competition and are viewed as a feature of physical instruction. They have existed as such through the ages. Essentially sports are singular exercises resulting from normal desire for development. Accordingly, sports are an integral part of human just as creature life.

Psychology of sports is a part of psychology that looks at different parts of sports exercises and physical culture. It likewise considers the psychological parts of the competitor's character. It creates analytic strategies for choosing individual of explicit sporting occasion and compelling training techniques. Sports psychology inspects the competitor's clairvoyant states in different complex circumstances. It likewise builds up the psychological establishments of sporting abilities by teaching ideal locomotor propensities and appropriate control of one's body and by encouraging the competitor's determination dry all round improvement.

Current sport; psychology has widened significantly from the early spotlight on motor learning, discernment and biomechanics. This incorporates motor abilities, learning, character, uneasiness and stress, struggle and competition, nonexistent training, unwinding training, consideration training, inspiration, socialization, advancement, group building, play and recreation, mental training, instructing, directing and wellness.

The essential meaning of the sports psychology is an investigation of behavior as it identifies with sports and motor capacity. (Petrosky, (1985), Robet N. Vocalist 1972). Also, sports psychology clarifies one's behavior in athletics. It likewise depicts the intelligent connection between motor test and gathering. An intuitive performance quality that exists in athletes encourages relational exertion. This "intelligent quality" has been investigated for a very long while (Comrey, 1953 Cornrey <wd Baskin, 1954; 1954, Weist, Portes and Grisell, 1961), Motor test were utilized that deliberate both individual endeavors and performance including the co-activity of at any rate two individuals. Hardly any investigations have been finished concerning the connection among individual and collective endeavors in motor test. These examinations have included co-relating the scores got from single subjects with scores created when those subjects interfaced with others on similar undertakings.

The sports performance is characterized as "a solidarity of execution and aftereffect of sports activity or an intricate arrangement of sports activity estimated or assessed by concurred and socially decided standards (Schnable, 1987) The performance is absolutely affected by the everyday environment of the life. This denotes the distinction in the degrees of performance of people. In this way it is obviously that sports performance is an exceptionally particular occasion which is being impacted by a few factors - social, financial, individual. As such, the performance is the psycho interaction. The idea of sports performance can simply by saw totally by examining this cycle. The investigation of this interaction will yield significant data about the construction of performance.

Accordingly, the current examination makes an endeavor to survey the impact of psychological factors like aggression and self concept on the motor test performance in 100 meters, 200 meters, and 400 meters run. The sample was selected from Gulbarga. The sample was likened as far as age and sex. In the primary stage, the sample having a place with age and sex was in his capacity to perform high.

Results have plainly shown the way that the performance of high aggressive respondents is fundamentally high than those of low aggression partners on the whole the three occasions of motor test. Along these lines the high aggression test is found to accomplish all the more generally.

Also, the present study assessed the role of the independent variables such as aggression, self concept, age and sex on the three motor tests of 100 meters, 200 meters and 400 meters. It uncovered the way that all these free factor have huge job on the sports performance. The investigation completely showed that all the psycho factors have solid relationship with the motor test performance on the whole the three track occasions.

Conclusions:

The major findings of present study are as follows

1. There is a significant, sex contrast in the measure of aggression: males are more aggressive than females.

2. The male players have significantly higher self-concept than those of female players.

3. Young competitors (youngsters) have altogether higher aggression than their partners.

4. The respondents of the age group-2 (seniors), have significantly higher self-concept than their partners.

5. There are significant differences in performances between the two samples sub-groups aggression: high aggressive players outperformed the other players on all three motor tests.

6. There is a significant or substantial difference in motor test results between two sub-groups of self concept. High self concept respondents performed substantially better on all three motor tests of 100 meters, 200 meters, and 400 meters than low self concept respondents. Psychological factors such as anger and self-concept have a major independent impact on athletic success in the 100-meter dash.

7. Psychological factors such as aggression and self-concept have a major independent impact on athletic success in the 100-meter dash.

8. There are significant gender disparities in athletic success, with males scoring substantially higher on all motor tests than females.

9. Athletes' motor efficiency in the 100 meters motor skill test is influenced by factors such as age and sex.

10. Psychological factors such as aggression and self-concept have a direct impact on players' success in the 200-meter game.

11. The efficiency of the motor in the 200 meter motor skill test was significantly and independently affected by factors such as age and sex.

12. Each psycho factor, such as aggression and self-concept, has affected the players' success in the 400-meter sprint independently and significantly.

13. Age and sex have a major and independent impact on motor capacity in the 400 meter run.

14. Psychological factors have an interaction influence on players' athletic success in all three motor test cases.

15. Psychological factors such as anger and self-concept have a positive and significant impact on motor test success in all three events: 100 meters, 200 meters, and 400 meters.

Suggestion and Recommendations

1. The result of the investigation would have been even seriously promising and pronouncing if statistical methodology like multiple examination and multiple regression investigation were utilized to evaluate the commitment of every independent variable to the dependent variable. This requires a further broadened examination that will be taken up.

2. Had the investigation contrasted the other athletic skills along and the current motor performance, it would have been even more extensive and generalizeable.

3. The investigation has not taken the team events for correlation which would have been more reasonable for examination of sports performance in connection with kick the bucket psycho factor contemplated, which will-be attempted in future research augmentation.

BIBLIOGRAPHY

Alderman, R.B. (1974). Psychological Behavior in Sport, Philadelphia W.B. Sounders.

Anderson, M.R. (1977). A study of the relationship between life satisfaction and self-concept, locus of control, satisfaction with primary relationship and work satisfaction. (Doctoral dissertation, Michgan State University, Dissertation, No. 77-25, 214).

Bandura, A. (1973). Aggression: A Social Learning Analysis. Engle Wood Cliffs, N.J.: Prentice-Hall.

Bandura, A. (1983). Psychological Mechanisms of Aggression, In R.G. Green and E.I. Donnostein (Eds), Aggression: Theoretical and Empirical Reviews: Vol.1, New York: Academic Press.

Baron, R.A. (1977) Human Aggression. New York: Plenum Press.

Baron, R.A. (1977). Human aggression. New York, Plenum Press.

Baron, R.A. and Ball, R.L. (1974). In R.A. Baron and Byrne (1981). Social Psychology: Understanding Human Interaction, 3rd Edition, Allyn and Bacon.

Berkowitz, L. (1969). Roots of Aggression. New York, Atherton Press.

Berkowitz, L. (1983). Aversively Stimulated Aggression: Some Parallels and Differences in Research with Animals and Humans, Amev can Psychologists, Vol. 38, PP. 1135-1144.

Binford, S. (1972). Apes and Original Sin. Human Behavior, 1 (6), 64-71.

Bjorkqvist Kaj, Orterman Karin (1992) Parental Influence of Children's Estimated Aggressiveness, Aggressive Behavior, Vol. 18 (6) PP. 411 —

Boren, R. (1977). Human Aggression. Plenum, New York.

Bousha, D.M. and Twentymen, C.T. (1984). Mother-Child International Sty ie in Abuse, Neglect and Control Groups: Naturalistic Observations ir the Home, Journal of Abnormal Psychology, Vol. 93, PP. 106-114.
Brook and Whiting (1975): "H.T.A. Human Movement A Field of Study1 Henry Kimption Publishers, London. .

Brunner, B.C. (1969). Personality and Motivating Factors Influencing Adult Participation n Vigorous Physical Activity. Research Quarterly, 46.

Buss, A.H. (1961). Psychology of Aggression. New York; Wiley.

Buss, A.H. (1966). Instrumentality of Aggression, Feedback, and Frustration as Determination of Physical Aggression, Journal of Personality and Social Psychology, Vol. 3, PP. 153-162.

Caplan, G. (1974). Support Systems and Community Mental Health. New York, Behavioral Publications.

Chandra, P.S., Sudha, M.B., Subbarathna, Shivaji Rao, Mathew Verghese and Channabasavanna, S.M. (1995). Mental Health in Mothers from af Traditional Society: The Role of Spouse Supportiveness. Family Therapy, Vol. 22, No. 1,PP. 49-59.

Colbert, Kent, R. (1993). The Effects of Debate Participation on Argumentativeness and Verbal Aggression, Communication Education July, Vol. 42 (3), PP. 206-214.

Collias, N. (1944) Aggressive Behavior: Vertebrate Animals, Psychological Zoology, Vol. 17, PP. 83-123.

Donnerstein, E., and Wilson, D.W. (1976). Effect of Noise and Perceived Control on Ongoing and Subsequent Aggressive Behavior, Journal of Personality and Social Psychology, Vol. 34, PP. 774-781.

Eagly, A.H. and Stef-fen, V.J. (1986). Gender and Aggression Behavior: A Meta-Analytic Rev.ew of the Social Psychological Literature, Psychological Bulletin, Vol. 100, PP. 309-300.

Feshbach, S. (1980). Child Abuse and the Dynamics of Human Aggression and Violence. In J. Gerbner, C.J. Ross and E. Zigler (Eds), Child Abuse: An agenda for Ac :ion. New York; Oxford University Press.

Flanagan, J.C. (1978). A Research Approach to Improving Quality of Life. American Psychologist, 33, PP. 138-147.

Fletcher, R. (1971). Relationships between Personality Traits and High School Activity Participation. Psychology. 8, 40-43.

Freedmen, J.L., (1975). Crowding and Behavior. San Francisco: W.H. Freeman.

Freud, S. (1920). A general introduction of Psycho-Analysis. New York; Boni and Liveright.

Frodi, A., Macaulay, J., and Thome, P.R. (1977) Are Women alway ess Aggressive than Men? A Review of the Experimental Literature, Psychological Bulletin, Vol. 84, PP. 634-660.

Frost, R.B. (1970). Psychological Concepts.Applied to Physical Education and Coaching, Massachsetts: Addison Wesley.

Gary Linn, J. and McGranahan, D;A. (1980). Personal Disruptions, Social Integration, Subjective Well-being and Predisposition Toward the Use of Counseling Services. American Journal of Community Psychology, Vol. 8, PP. 87-100.

Gladue Brain (1991). Aggressive Behavior Characteristics, Harmones, and Sexual Orientation in Men and Women, Aggressive Behavior; Vol. 17 (6), PP. 313-326.

Gourash Nancy (1978). Help-seeking: A Review of Literature. American Journal of Community Psychology, Vol. 6, No. 5, PP. 413-423.

Gray, E.B., Megan, C Lovejoy, Chaya, S. Piotrkowski and James, T. bond (1990). Husband Supportiveness and the Well-being of Employed Mothers of Infants, Families in Society. The Journal of Contemporary Human Services^ 7, PP. 332-341.

Green, R.G., and O'Neal, E.C. (1976). Perspectives on Aggression. New Academic Press.

Gurin, G., Veroff, J. ard Field, S. (1960). Americans View their Mental He; New York, Basic Books.

Hall, C.S. and Lindzey, G. (1957). Introduction to Theories of Personality, i York: John Wile / and Sons.

Heller, Kenneth and Mansbach, W.E. (1984). The Multi-faceted Nature of Sociai Support in a Community Sample of Elderly Women. Journal of Social Issues., Vol. 40, No. 4, PP. 99-112.

Hirsch, B.J. (1980). Natural Support Systems and Coping with Major Changes. Amerban Journal of Community Psychology, Vol. 8, No. 2. PP. 159-172.

Jacobs, P.A., Brunton. M. and Melville, M.M. (1965), Aggressive Behavior, Mental Subnormally and the XYY male, Nature (London), Vol. 208, PP. 1351-1352.

Jarvik, L.F., Kloden, V; and Matsuyana, S.S. (1973). Human Aggression and the "Extra Y chromosome; Fact or Fantasy? American Psychologist, Vol. 28, PP. 674-682.

Johnson, Hutlan, (1954). Personality Traits of Some Champion Athleies as Measured by Two Projective Test. Research and H.T.P. Research Quarterly, 25, P 484.

Kaufmann, H. (1970). Aggression and Altruism, New York, Holt, Rinehari and Winston.

Kundu, Ramanath; Cheudhuri Jayanti R. (1989). Effect of Some Psycho-S Variables on Verbal Aggression Generated by Frustration, Pharmacopsychcescologia Vol. 2 (1-2), PP. 63-68.

Lansky, L.M., Crandall, V.J., Kagan, J., and Baker, C.T. (1961). Sex Differences in Aggression and its Correlates in Middle Class Adolescents, Child Development, Vol. 34, PP. 45-58.

Lloyd, C.W., and Weisz, J. (1975). Harmonies and Aggression. In W.S. Fields, and W.H. Sweet (Eds), Neural Bases of Violence and Aggression. PP 92-113. St. Louis: Warren H. Green.

Maccoby, E.E. and Jacklin, C.N. (1974). The Psychology of Sex Differences. Stanford, CA., S :anford University Press.

Mahamood, M. (1981). Personality Profiles of Sportsman and Non-sportsmen. Psychological Stidies. 26 (1), 5-7.

Mc Cabe Allyssa, Lipscomb Thomas, J. (1988) Sex Differences in Children's Verbal Aggression, Merrill Palmer Quarterly, Oct, Vol. 34 (4), PP. 389-401.

Moore, Robert, A., (1956). Sport and Mental Health, Springfield, Illinois, Charts C. Thomas.

Morgon, W.P. (1979). Prediction of Performance in Athletics. In : Klavora, P. and Daniel, J.D. (Eds.) Coach, Athlete and the Sport Psychologist University of Toronto, Toronto, Canada, PP. 173-186.

Moyer, K.E. (1976). The Psychology of Aggression, New York: Harpei and Row.

Murrell, S.A. and Nonis, F.H. (1984). Resources, Life Events, and Changes in Positive Affect and Depression in Older Adults. American Journal of Community Psychology, Vol. 12, No. 4, PP. 445-464.

Nolen, Hoeksema, Susan (1994). An Interactive Model for the Emergence of Gender Difference in Depression in Adolescence, Special Issue: Affective Process in Adolescence, Journal of Research on Adolescence. Vol. PP. 519-534.

Ogilvie, B.C. and Tuttco, T.A. (1971). "Personality". Encyclopedia of Sports Sciences and Medicine. New York, Macmillan, 229-233.

Oritt, E.J., Stephen, C. Paul and Jay A. Behrman. (1985). The Perceived Social Network Inventory, American Journal of Community Psychology, Voi. 13, No. 5, PP. 565-582.

Patterson, G.R. (1976). The Aggressive Child: Victim and Architect of a Coercive System In E.J. Marsh, L.A. Hamerlynck, and L.C. Handy (Eds). Behavior Modification and Families, New York: Brunner.

Peterson, S.L. (1967). Personality Traits of Women in Team Sports, Versus Women in Individual Sports, Research Quarterly, 38, 52-60.

Petrovsky, A.V. and Ycroshevsky, (1985). A Concise Psychological Dictionary. Moscow, Progres s Publishers.

Prasad, S.C. (1980). Differences in Expression of Aggression, Asian Journal of Psychology.and Education, Vol. 6 (2) PP. 33-35.

Rajeski, W. (1980). Causal Attribution: An Aid to Understanding and Motivating Athletics. Motor skills : Theory into Practice, 4, 32-36.

Riley, J.H. (1983). Thz Relationship between Physical Estimation, Phy^ Performance and Self concept for Sixth Grade Boys and Girls. DAI, 4

Robert, E.L. Roberts and Vern, L. Bengtson (1993). Relationship with Parents, Self-esteem and Psychological Well-being in Young Adulthood. Social Psychology Quatterly, Vol. 56, No. 4, PP. 263-277.

Robert, N. Singer, (IS72). Coaching Athletics and Psychology, New York, McGrawhill, P. 177.

Roberts, G.C. (1975\ Win-loss Attributions of Little-Leagus Players. Movement, 7, 315-322.

Rogers, C.R. (1951). Client Centered Therapy: Its Current Practice, Implication and Theory, Boston, Pub.

Rotter, J.B. (1966). Generalized Expectancies for Internal Versus Ext Control of Reinforcement. Psychological Monographs, 80, 1-15.

Rozario, J; Kapur, M. Rao, Shivaji, Dalai, M. (1994). A Comparative Study of Prevalence and Pattern of Psychological Disturbances of Adolescent and Girls. Special Section: Frustration, Adjustment and Psychological Disturbance, Journal of Personality and Clinical Studies: Mar-Sep. Vol. 10 (1-2), PP. 65-70.

Rubenstein, Judith, Feldman, S.S., Rubin Carol and Noveck, Ira. (1987). A Cross-Cultural Comparison of Children's Drawing of some Mixed Sex Pear Interaction, Journal of Cross-Cultural Pyschology. Vol. 18 (2), PP. 234-250.

Salokun, (1990). Comparison of Nigerian High School Male Athletes and Non-athletes on Sell* Concept, Perceptual and Motor Skills. Psychological Reports, Vol. 70, 865-866.

Sandler, I.N. and Barrera M. Jr. (1984). Toward a Multi-method Approach to Assessing the Effect of Social Support. American Journal of Community Psychology, Vo . 12, No. 1, PP. 37-52.

Schedel, J. (1965). Psychological Differences between Athletes and Non-participants in Athletics at Three Educational Levels. Research Quarterly, 36, 52-67.

Schnabel, (1981). "Die Rolle Ler Sports Medizim Bei Der Sportlichen Eignumgrstic, Ir. Theoric and Praxis Der Korper Kuture.

Scott, Henderson, Byrne, D.G., Duncan, Jones, P., Sylvia, Adcock, Ruth Scott, and Steele, G.P. (1978a). Social Bonds in the Epidemiology of Neurosis: A Preliminary Communication. British Journal of Psychiatry, Vol. 132, PP. 463-466.

Scott, Henderson, Paula Duncan Jones, Helen, McAuley and Karen, Ritchie (1978b). The Patient's Primary Group. British Journal of Psychiatry. Vol. 132, PP. 74-86.

Shivaramakrishnan, S. (1994). Sports Achievement Motivation, Self Concept and Anxiety Differentials Among Indian Men and Women Basketball and Volleyball Players Prior to S.A.F. Games. Journal of Physical Education 1 and Sports Sciences, Vol. 4, No. 1.

Terman, CM., and Tyler, L.E. (1954). Psychological Sex Differences, In L.Carmichael (Ed) Manual of Child Psychology. New York: John Wiley and Sons.

Thoits, P.A. (1982). Conceptual, Methodological and Theoretical Problems in Studying Social Support as a Buffer against Life Stress. Journal of H al h and Social Behavior, 23, PP. 145-159.

Tieger, T. (1980). On the Biological basis of Sex Differences in Aggression. Child Development, Vol. 51, PP. 943-963.

Vaux, A. and Harrison Deborah- (1985). Support Network Characteristics Associated with Support Satisfaction and Perceived Support. American Journal of Community Psychology, Vol. 13, No. 3, PP. 245-268.

Vaux, A., Jeffrey Philips, Lori Holly, Brian Thomson, Deirdre Williams and Doren Stewart (1986). The Social Support Appraisals (SS-A) Scale. Studies of Reliability and Validity. American Journal of Community Psychology, Vol. 14, No. 2, PP. 195-219.

Verchosankij (1971). "Grundlagen Des Speziellon Kraft Training in Sports. In Theoric and Praxis Der Korperkulture, Beiheft.

Volkamer, M. (1971). Zurur Aggressivitat in Konkumenz Orientation Sozialen, Sport Wissenschaft, 1, 68-72.

Wasserman, G.A., Green, A., and Allen, R. (1983). Going Beyond abuse; Maladaptive Patterns of Interaction in Abusing Mother-Infant Pairs, Journal of the American Academy of Child Psychiatry, Vol. 22. PP. 245-252.

Wethington, E. and Kessler, R.C. (1986). Perceived Support, Received Support and Adjustment to Stressful Life Events. Journal of Health and Social Behavior, 27, PP. 78-89.

White, R.W. (1959). Motivation Revisited: The Concept of Competence. Psychological Review, 66, PP. 297-333.

Zautra, A. (1983). Social Resources and the Quality of Life. American Journal of Community Psychology, Vol. 11, No. 3, PP. 275-290.

CPSIA information can be obtained
at www.ICGtesting.com
Printed in the USA
LVHW051235080123
736584LV00007B/226

9 783262 578449